Sound Practice in Government Debt Management

Sound Practice in Government Debt Management

Graeme Wheeler

THE WORLD BANK

Library of Congress Cataloging-in-Publication Data

Wheeler, Graeme, 1951-
  Sound practice in government debt management / Graeme Wheeler.
    p. cm.
  Includes bibliographical references and index.
  ISBN 0-8213-5073-0
    1. Debts, Public—Management. I. Title.

HJ8015.W48 2003
352.4'5—dc22

Table of Contents

Foreword

Governments around the world face a complex array of competing economic and policy demands in seeking to improve the lives of their citizens. Peoples of these nations seek additional and improved services for education, health care, social justice, and security, as well as more efficient and equitable systems of taxation. At the same time, to ensure that development is durable and to reduce the risk of debilitating crises, many governments need to strengthen their fiscal discipline, improve the quality of public debt management, and address the rapid growth of contingent liabilities arising from weak banking systems and poor governance practices. The interplay of these tensions takes us into the heart of political economy, where decisions may well have profound effects on growth, productivity, and income distribution.

Helping to meet these challenges through sound government debt management is important for the smallest Heavily Indebted Poor Countries as well as the major economies. A government's debt portfolio is usually the largest financial portfolio in the country. It often contains complex exposures that create substantial risk for the government and the country's financial stability—particularly where large amounts of foreign-currency debt and short-term debt are involved.

Prudent government debt management has critical linkages to the development process. It reduces the financial risk the government faces, lowers the economy's vulnerability to financial shocks, strengthens the market infrastructure and institutions needed to support an efficient domestic financial market, and helps foster sound public sector governance practices.

This book is directed to policy makers and advisers who review their government debt management operations. It presents ideas and management insights drawn from the twin perspectives of theory and practice: the debt management literature as well as real-life experiences of the successes and failures in program development that countries have experienced.

I believe that the ideas in this book will be extremely useful for government debt managers and public policy advisors around the world.

James D. Wolfensohn
President
World Bank

Acknowledgments

Many of the ideas expressed in this book were developed through working with colleagues in the New Zealand Treasury, the New Zealand Debt Management office, and the World Bank Treasury. The New Zealand Treasury undertook pioneering work in governance and public sector management in the late 1980s and the 1990s; the New Zealand Debt Management Office conducted conceptual and empirical analysis placing debt management strategy in the broader framework of government asset and liability management. This thinking was further developed by colleagues in the public debt management group in the World Bank Treasury.

I would like to express particular thanks to Fred Jensen, who is a senior advisor in the public debt management group. Fred and I worked closely in partnering with Robert Price, Piero Ugolini, and Mark Zelmer in the International Monetary Fund and with government debt managers in member countries to produce the World Bank/International Monetary Fund *Guidelines for Public Debt Management*; a copy is included as Annex 2. Fred's clear thinking has been a great help in writing the book, and it has been especially important in the preparation of the chapters focusing on managing government debt in an asset and liability framework, developing a risk management framework and contingent liabilities.

I also am extremely grateful to Eriko Togo for her hard work in obtaining data and for her numerous suggestions and contributions on ways to improve the book, and to Phillip Anderson, who also made valuable comments on the final draft. Both Eriko and Phillip work in the public debt management group.

Colleagues from the public debt management group and the banking and capital markets department in the World Bank Treasury commented on an early draft, and I wish to thank Ravi Balasubramanian, Krishnan Chandresakhar, Elizabeth Currie, Doris Herrera-Pol, Lars Jessen, Kenneth

Lay, Tomas Magnusson, Sam Pal, Stefan Piot, Hiroshi Tsubota, Antonio Velandia-Rubiano, Pierre Yourougou, and Ivan Zelenko.

I also benefited considerably from comments received on an early draft from numerous government debt managers. In particular, I am grateful for the comments received from Fabio Barbosa, former head of the Brazilian Treasury, and Paul Tucker, Executive Director, Markets, in the Bank of England.

I am very appreciative of the generosity of my senior management friends in the World Bank Treasury—Myles Brennan, Antonio Ferreira, John Gandolfo, Kenneth Lay, and Gumersindo Oilveros—and Gary Perlin, former Chief Financial Officer in the World Bank, for their unfailing support while I wrote the book.

Last, and far from least, I wish to thank my editors, Nancy Levine and Mary Fisk. Nancy had wonderful ideas on improving the text and context, and Mary managed the whole production process.

About the Author

Graeme Wheeler has been Vice President and Treasurer of the World Bank since July 2001. He joined the World Bank in 1997 as Director of the Financial Products and Services Department. For the previous four years, he was the Treasurer of the New Zealand Debt Management Office and a Deputy Secretary to the New Zealand Treasury. Prior to this, he was Director of Macroeconomic Policy and Forecasting in the New Zealand Treasury. During the second half of the 1980s, Graeme Wheeler was the Economic Counselor for the New Zealand Delegation to the Organisation for Economic Co-operation and Development in Paris.

Chapter 1

An Overview of Government Debt Management

Government debt management has a long tradition. More than three centuries ago, the Bank of England was managing government debt, and the origins of Sweden's National Debt Office go back to 1789.[1] In recent years, there has been a move toward building the professionalism of government debt management, beginning with the establishment of the New Zealand Debt Management Office in 1988 and Ireland's National Treasury Management Agency in 1990.

RECENT MOVES TOWARD IMPROVED DEBT MANAGEMENT

It is no accident that the countries that were the first to substantially upgrade their government debt management in the late 1980s and early 1990s were those with histories of fiscal problems, high ratios of public sector debt to gross domestic product (GDP), and a large proportion of foreign currency debt in their government debt portfolios.[2] These same features are characteristic of many developing countries today. Concern over rising government indebtedness has been a factor behind debt management reforms in Brazil, China, Colombia, India, the Republic of Korea, Mexico, South Africa, and Thailand, and it helps explain why several other governments, including those of Jordan, Lebanon, and Peru, are considering extensive reforms in government debt management.

Prior to the introduction of comprehensive government debt management reforms in the late 1980s and the 1990s, government debt was frequently "managed" without clear objectives or a supporting policy framework. Financing decisions were often politically motivated or were based on achieving the lowest annual debt-servicing cost regardless of portfolio risk. An integrated approach to debt management was rare. Management of government debt was fractured, being split across a myriad of government agencies (including the central bank), all of which vigorously protected their interests. These difficulties were compounded by rapid debt accumulation by state-owned enterprises, large debt portfolios at subnational levels, and a wide range of contingent liabilities entered into by the government.

Since the late 1980s, several factors have stimulated efforts to take a more professional approach toward management of government debt. One was the growing recognition among early reformers such as Ireland, New Zealand, and Sweden that the structure of government debt, not just its level, was important and that poor-quality decisions on government debt management added to the overall riskiness of the government's balance sheet. Another was the increased understanding that a prudent debt management strategy, along with sound macroeconomic and structural adjustment policies, is essential for containing the impact of financial market shocks, regardless of whether they are domestic in origin or the result of global financial market contagion.

The East Asian financial crisis of 1997–98 and its aftermath illustrate how the interaction of exchange rate policy, the tax regime, and financial sector regulation can create incentives for excessive risk taking. Poor asset and liability management practices in financial intermediaries resulted in governments' having to inject capital into publicly owned banks and assume private sector financial obligations. Assignment of a high priority to the strengthening of the quality of government debt management was a key element of the policy reform packages in Korea and Thailand.

Interest in improving the quality of government debt management was a natural corollary of broader reforms. In the early 1980s, many member countries of the Organisation for Economic Co-operation and Development (OECD) undertook extensive reforms aimed at improving economic management. Initially, the focus was on reducing macroeconomic imbalances and on deregulation of factor and product markets.[3] Initiatives to review government ownership interests and improve the efficiency of the delivery of publicly produced goods and services tended to come later. These latter measures included privatization and corporatization of state-owned enterprises; reviews of contingent and off-budget liabilities; widespread public sector accounting, budgeting, and human resource reforms; and institutional reforms designed to improve accountability for the delivery and quality of a wide range of public goods. In an environment in which ratios of net government debt to GDP were often well above 75 percent and annual debt-servicing costs accounted for more than 20 percent of tax revenue, policymakers' attention turned to improving the quality of government debt management.

Deregulation of the financial sector and innovations in financial products also played an important role. Deregulation of domestic financial markets assisted the development of domestic debt markets and allowed for the separation of monetary policy from government debt management and for the clarification of accountabilities for monetary policy and debt management policy. Government debt managers were able to pursue their cost and risk objectives by issuing debt instruments in the primary market, and central banks could achieve their monetary policy goals by buying and selling government securities in the secondary market or through other policy instruments that did not rely on interventions in the primary market.

Globally, financial sector reform, including the removal of capital controls, led to increased international capital flows and the development of a broader range of financial products to manage the growing volatility in interest rates, exchange rates, and commodity prices. Governments were confronted with an array of new borrowing and hedging products in financial markets that could enable them to manage financial risk by altering the cost and risk characteristics of their asset and liability portfolios. They needed specialists who knew how these instruments could be applied to help meet public policy goals and who understood the benefits and risks associated with their application. Also required were legal and systems expertise and staffs with accounting and settlement skills.

Investor pressures helped catalyze debt management reforms. Investors, particularly foreign ones, stressed that in order to invest in government securities markets, they required transparent and consistent government debt management strategies, equal treatment for all investor groups, comprehensive disclosure of the government's financial position, commitments by the government to build liquidity in government benchmark securities, and an efficient financial market infrastructure for transactions.

More subtle, but also important, was the country peer pressure that led policy advisers and decisionmakers to review carefully the approaches that other countries were adopting in their government debt management.[4] In

Latin American countries such as Brazil, Colombia, and Mexico, peer effects from debt management reforms in OECD countries were influential in raising awareness of the importance of sound public debt management practices. Another important factor was the effect of debt renegotiations (e.g., within the Paris Club and the HIPC initiative) in demonstrating the need for competent debt managers.

To sum up, broad financial sector deregulation and the product innovation and policy demands by global investors that accompanied it created risks and opportunities for government balance sheet management that were quite different from those that government debt managers had traditionally faced. Governments needed more specialized debt management advice and transaction expertise.

WHAT IS GOVERNMENT DEBT MANAGEMENT?

Government debt management is the process of establishing and implementing a strategy for prudently managing the government's debt in order to meet the government's financing needs, its cost and risk objectives, and any other debt management goals the government may have set, such as developing and maintaining an efficient market for government securities. The aim of debt management is to ensure that the government's borrowing needs are met efficiently and that the stock of government debt, and the incremental debt flows arising from budget and off-budget sources, are managed in a manner consistent with the government's cost and risk preferences.

In essence, the process of government debt management mainly entails:

- Establishing clear debt management objectives and supporting them with a sound governance framework, a prudent cost and risk management strategy and accompanying portfolio management policies; an efficient organizational structure; appropriate management information systems; and a strong in-house risk management culture

- Ensuring that all portfolio-related transactions are consistent with the government's debt management strategy and are executed as efficiently as possible

- Establishing reporting procedures to ensure that the government's debt managers are accountable for implementing the debt management responsibilities delegated to them.

At a minimum, a government debt management strategy should cover all of the domestic and foreign currency debt obligations of the central government. In some situations it may cover broader public sector liabilities, including the debt of state-owned enterprises and debt guaranteed by the government. Increasingly, government debt managers monitor (and sometimes manage) the risk exposures associated with explicit contingent liabilities of the government, such as underwriting commitments and guarantees.[5]

HOW DOES GOVERNMENT DEBT MANAGEMENT DIFFER FROM OTHER DIMENSIONS OF MACROECONOMIC MANAGEMENT?

Government debt managers and fiscal policy advisers have similar concerns, but often their goals are different. Government debt managers examine the structure of the government's portfolio of debt and the changes in it (which may be a result of financing decisions associated with fiscal policy) with a view to ensuring that the expected cost and risk of the debt portfolio remain within tolerances acceptable to the government. Fiscal policy, by contrast, is usually concerned with the effects of aggregate government spending and taxation on a range of macroeconomic variables and with the microeconomic impacts of individual tax and spending policies on resource allocation, welfare, and economic growth.

Nevertheless, government debt managers and fiscal policy advisers share many concerns. Both want the government to adopt prudent borrowing practices, meet all repayment obligations on time, and maintain a sound portfolio structure for its debt. They also advocate the adoption of a credible fiscal strategy to ensure that current and projected levels of public sector indebtedness remain on a sustainable path, and the introduction of measures to manage the government's balance sheet risks associated with contingent liabilities.

As is discussed in chapter 2, there are also important links between debt management policy and monetary policy. These connections are illustrated by the choices governments face as to how to finance budget deficits and manage the daily liquidity flows between the government and the banking system that arise from the government's financial transactions (which include budgetary flows and any receipts from privatization).

In countries with less developed bond markets, the same short-dated instruments in the primary market are often used both to conduct monetary policy and to finance the government's borrowing needs. In these situations, considerable cooperation and information sharing between the ministry of finance and the central bank are necessary. Increasingly, governments see considerable benefits in developing separate and transparent goals for monetary policy and debt management policy and in establishing clear accountabilities and institutional arrangements that reinforce the independence of the policy domains.

A government's exchange rate policy can also have important implications for its debt management, especially with regard to the design of strategic benchmarks, which specify the desired currency composition of the government's foreign currency debt and guide new foreign currency borrowing decisions. As is discussed in chapter 4, many governments are looking for ways in which government assets and liabilities can be structured so as to reduce the government's overall balance sheet risk.[6]

WHY IS GOVERNMENT DEBT MANAGEMENT IMPORTANT?

Although most governments have significant levels of debt to manage, prudent government debt management is especially important in emerging market countries. Governments in these countries often face considerable balance sheet risk, given their high levels of indebtedness in relation to GDP and to export receipts, their economies' dependence on commodities, and their exposure to volatile terms of trade movements and capital flows. At the same time, their domestic capital markets may be fragile; the process of fiscal decentralization is often at a formative stage; and an extensive array of guarantees and other contingent obligations needs to be managed.[7]

Prudent government debt management is important for several reasons. A government's debt portfolio is usually the largest financial portfolio in the country.[8] It often contains complex and risky financial structures, and it can generate substantial risk to the government's balance sheet and to the country's financial stability. Government debt-servicing costs are often very high, and because making timely debt servicing payments is a priority for governments, they can reduce the volume of resources available for other uses. It is not unusual, for example, to see annual government debt servicing costs exceed a government's total spending on health and education.

High-quality government debt management can help lower a government's debt-servicing costs by reducing the credit premium and the liquidity premium in the term structure of interest rates for government securities. Although the quality of government debt management may not necessarily, by itself, lead to a higher credit assessment by the financial markets or the sovereign credit rating agencies, it can contribute to such a rating, especially when accompanied by prudent fiscal and monetary policies. Poor debt management practices have frequently been cited by the sovereign credit rating agencies in announcing sovereign downgrades. Since a government's sovereign credit rating usually establishes a ceiling on the credit ratings of other domestic entities, a higher sovereign rating can create scope for reassessing other domestic borrowers.[9] If, on the other hand, the government's debt management strategy is poorly designed, implemented, and communicated, it can induce adverse investor sentiment, raise debt-servicing costs, damage the government's reputation, and exacerbate financial market instability.

Management of expected cost and risk in the debt portfolio

Table 1 summarizes the types of risk that debt managers face.

Table 1: Risks encountered in management of government debt

Risk	Description
Market risk	Risks associated with changes in market prices, such as interest rates, exchange rates, and commodity prices. For both domestic and foreign currency debt, changes in interest rates affect debt-servicing costs on new issues when fixed-rate debt is refinanced and on floating-rate debt at the rate reset dates. Hence, short-duration (short-term or floating-rate) debt is usually considered riskier than long-term, fixed rate debt. (Excessive concentration in very long term fixed-rate debt can also be risky, as future financing requirements are uncertain.) Debt denominated in or indexed to foreign currencies also adds volatility to debt-servicing costs as measured in domestic currency, owing to exchange rate movements. Bonds with embedded put options can exacerbate market risk.
Rollover risk	The risk that debt will have to be rolled over at an unusually high cost or, in extreme cases, that it cannot be rolled over at all. To the extent that rollover risk means only that debt might have to be rolled over at higher interest rates, including adverse changes in credit spreads, it may be considered a type of market risk. But in fact, it is often treated separately because inability to roll over debt, or exceptionally large increases in government funding costs, can lead to or exacerbate a debt crisis and thereby cause real economic losses, in addition to the purely financial effects of higher interest rates. Managing rollover risk is particularly important for emerging market countries.

(Table continues on the following page.)

Table 1: (continued)

Risk	Description
Liquidity risk	There are two types of liquidity risk. One refers to the cost or penalty investors face in trying to exit a position when the number of transactors has markedly decreased or a particular market is lacking in depth. This risk is particularly relevant in cases where debt management includes the management of liquid assets or the use of derivatives contracts. The other form of liquidity risk, for a borrower, refers to a situation in which the volume of liquid assets can diminish quickly because of unanticipated cash flow obligations or difficulties in raising cash through borrowing within a short period of time.
Credit risk	The risk of nonperformance by borrowers on loans or other financial assets or by a counterparty in financial contracts. This risk is particularly germane in cases where debt management includes the management of liquid assets. It may also be relevant in the acceptance of bids in auctions of securities issued by the government, in relation to contingent liabilities, and in derivatives contracts entered into by the debt manager.
Settlement risk	Refers to the potential loss that the government could suffer as a result of failure by the counterparty to settle, for whatever reason other than default.
Operational risk	Includes a range of risks, such as errors in the various stages of executing and recording transactions; inadequacies or failures in internal controls or in systems and services; reputational risk; legal risk; security breaches; or natural disasters that affect business activity.

Source: World Bank and IMF 2001.

Box 1 outlines some of the pitfalls that debt managers should guard against because they can significantly increase the expected cost and risk associated with the government's debt management.

Contribution to macroeconomic stability

Historically, risky government debt structures—characterized by excessive amounts of short-term or floating-rate debt, or of debt dominated in or indexed to foreign currencies—and the macroeconomic policies that necessitate these portfolio choices have been major factors in economic and financial crises. By reducing the risk that the government's own portfolio management will become a source of instability for the private sector, prudent debt management can help make countries less susceptible to contagion and financial risk.

A government debt management strategy that seeks to build a low-risk government debt portfolio by choosing an appropriate currency composition, interest rate structure, and maturity profile can help reduce the effects

Box 1
Some pitfalls in debt management

Some problems frequently encountered in government debt management are summarized below. Many of them arise from unclear objectives and weak governance arrangements, including poor accounting, disclosure, and reporting practices and inadequate oversight and control frameworks.

1. *Increasing the vulnerability of the government's financial position by accepting higher risk that may lead to lower costs and a lower deficit in the short run.* Debt managers should avoid exposing their portfolios to even low-probability risks of large or catastrophic losses in an effort to capture marginal cost savings. Some danger areas are:
   - *Maturity structure.* The intertemporal tradeoff between short-term and long-term costs should be managed prudently. For example, excessive reliance on short-term or floating-rate paper to take advantage of lower short-term interest rates may leave the government vulnerable to volatile and possibly rising debt-servicing costs if interest rates increase, and to the risk of default in the event that the government cannot roll over its debts at all. It could also affect the achievement of the central bank's monetary objectives.
   - *Excessive unhedged foreign exchange exposures.* This risk can take many forms, but the predominant one is when a government directly issues excessive amounts of debt denominated in or indexed to foreign currencies. This practice may leave governments vulnerable to volatile and possibly increasing debt-servicing costs if their exchange rates depreciate and to the risk of default if they cannot roll over their debts.
   - *Debt with embedded put options.* If poorly managed, these options increase uncertainty to the issuer, effectively shortening the portfolio duration and creating greater exposure to market or rollover risk.
   - *Implicit contingent liabilities,* such as implicit guarantees to financial institutions. If poorly managed, these liabilities tend to be associated with significant moral hazard.
2. *Debt management practices that distort private versus government decisions and that understate the true interest cost.* These include:
   - *Collaterization of debt by shares of state-owned enterprises or other assets.* In addition to understating the underlying interest cost, this practice may distort decisions regarding asset management.

(Box continues on the following page.)

Box 1 (continued)

- *Collaterization of debt by specific sources of future tax revenue.* If a future stream of revenue is committed for specific debt payments, the government may be less willing to undertake changes that affect this revenue, even if the changes would improve the tax system.
- *Tax-exempt or reduced-tax debt.* These incentives are used to encourage the placement of government debt. The impact on the deficit is ambiguous, since it will depend on the taxation of competing assets and on whether the after-tax rates of return on taxable and tax-exempt government paper are equalized.

3. *Misreporting of contingent or guaranteed debt liabilities,* which may understate the actual level of the government's liabilities. Problems include:
   - *Inadequate coordination or procedures* with regard to borrowing by lower levels of government that may be guaranteed by the central government, as well as borrowing by state-owned enterprises.
   - *Repeated debt forgiveness for lower levels of government or for state-owned enterprises.*
   - *Loan guarantees* that have a high probability of being called (if there are not appropriate budgetary provisions).

4. *Use of nonmarket financing channels,* which in some cases can be unambiguously distortionary:
   - *Special arrangements with the central bank for concessional credit,* including zero-interest or low-interest overdrafts or special treasury bills.
   - *Forced borrowing from suppliers,* through expenditure arrears, the issuance of promissory notes, and tied borrowing arrangements. These practices tend to raise the price of government expenditures.
   - *Creation of a captive market for government securities.* For example, the government pension plan may be required to buy government securities, or banks may be required to acquire government debt equivalent to a certain percentage of their deposits. Although some forms of liquid asset ratios can be useful prudential tools for liquidity management, they can have distortionary effects on debt-servicing costs, as well as on the development of financial markets.

5. *Improper oversight or recording of debt contracting and payment, and inadequate oversight of debtholders,* resulting in less government control of the tax base or of the supply of outstanding debt. Problems include:
   - *Failure to record implicit interest on zero-coupon long-term debt.* This practice may help the government's cash position, but it leads to understatement of the true deficit.

- *Too broad an authority to incur debt* as a result of lack of parliamentary reporting requirements on debt incurred or the absence of a borrowing limit or debt ceiling. (The authority, nevertheless, must ensure that existing debt service obligations are met.)
- *Inadequate controls on the amount of debt outstanding.* In some countries a breakdown in internal operations and poor documentation have led to more debt being issued than had been officially authorized.
- *Onerous legal requirements with respect to certain forms of borrowing.* In some countries more burdensome legal requirements for long-maturity relative to short-maturity borrowings have led to disproportionate reliance on the latter, which heightens rollover risk.

Source: World Bank and IMF 2001.

of financial shocks on the government's balance sheet. Adverse demand- and supply-side shocks, which affect output and inflation, also have a fiscal impact that can be offset in part by establishing a diversified set of domestic funding instruments. Such instruments may have financial characteristics that can help hedge the government's fiscal position against changes in government tax revenues and spending resulting from the shock. (See the discussion in chapter 4.)

Government debt management policies can have important implications for the effectiveness of macroeconomic policies and for other elements of government financial management. To the extent possible, the day-to-day implementation of sound debt management policies should seek to reinforce the objectives of macroeconomic policies and of policy reforms aimed at improving the efficiency of the domestic financial market. For example, debt management practices should seek to build investor participation in the domestic bond market and reduce uncertainty premia by ensuring that debt management goals and policies are clear and do not discriminate among classes of investors. Similarly, concentrating issuance on a limited number of government securities and building up their liquidity can help reduce the liquidity premium that investors price into government securities. Unfortunately, this type of reinforcement between debt management policy and other macroeconomic policy instruments is not always possible, and, as discussed in chapter 2, there can be significant policy conflicts among government debt managers, central bankers, and fiscal policy advisers.

Development of debt markets

In most countries, decisions by government debt managers as to which types of instruments to issue and the most appropriate issuance strategy and market infrastructure for supporting these instruments have been important catalysts in developing the overall structure of the domestic securities market. For example, policies aimed at establishing a liquid government yield curve help reduce transaction costs for other market participants by enabling them to price risk, form long-term contracts, and issue their own fixed-income securities. Such policies have been instrumental in supporting the development of repo and swap markets, as well as the futures and options markets. Government benchmark bonds can be a valuable hedging instrument for the private sector, provided that the bonds are liquid and that movements in the yields on private sector instruments correlate with those on government bonds. Establishing government benchmark issues in foreign currencies can assist the private sector in accessing the international capital markets in those currencies.

Protection of the government's reputation

The quality of government debt management can have important effects on a government's reputation. Government debt managers represent the minister of finance in financial markets. The professionalism with which they conduct their relationships with underwriters, investors, and rating agencies, and how they communicate on a range of public policy issues relating to the government's role in financial markets and its strategy for managing cost and risk, can affect the market's judgment of the government's financial management. Similarly, the government's role as a financial market participant is important in conveying messages to the financial markets about acceptable standards of behavior. It is essential, therefore, that the government's debt be managed according to the highest ethical standards.

Government debt managers need to protect their governments from the risks associated with international fraud. This risk should not be underestimated. It is not uncommon for government ministers and debt managers to be approached by individuals claiming to have access to very large foreign currency borrowing opportunities at highly subsidized rates in return for up-front fees or a letter of representation. These individuals may seek to use a ministerial letter or the official letterhead of a government debt office to help establish their credentials and defraud another borrower or investor. In some countries, banks and charitable institutions have lost millions of dollars through fraudulent investment deals involving what are known as prime bank notes.[10]

OBJECTIVES OF GOVERNMENT DEBT MANAGEMENT

The primary objectives of government debt management are to finance the government's borrowing needs efficiently and to ensure that the government's debt-servicing obligations are met. For governments with strong foreign currency credit ratings, accessing international markets is relatively straightforward, but it can become a major preoccupation for countries with small domestic capital markets that depend on foreign currency borrowing to help maintain their foreign currency reserves and finance their fiscal deficits.

As indicated in table 2, another main objective is to ensure that the government debt portfolio is managed according to the government's cost and risk objectives. Several OECD governments have set government debt management objectives aimed at minimizing the government's expected debt-servicing costs over the medium and longer term, subject to a prudent level of portfolio risk. Objectives for a number of (mostly OECD) government debt offices are outlined in table 2.

Governments may also have secondary objectives, such as maintaining the liquidity of government issues at various points on the yield curve in order to reduce liquidity premia and provide a pricing benchmark for private issuers. Emerging market countries may seek to promote the development of the domestic debt market through a gradual extension of the maturities of government debt and the introduction of new debt instruments.

A goal of minimizing debt-servicing cost, irrespective of risk, should not be an explicit objective. This strategy can result in riskier borrowing structures and an increased danger that adverse shocks could result in higher debt-servicing costs, leading to higher taxes, reduced government services, or even outright default.

Financial crises and sovereign defaults have often occurred because governments have focused solely on expected cost savings (through, for example, issuance of large volumes of short-term debt). The consequences can be that government budgets are seriously exposed to changing financial market conditions, including investors' reassessments of the country's creditworthiness and the effects of global contagion. These adjustments are often reflected in sharply higher government borrowing costs and currency

Table 2: Primary objectives of government debt management for selected countries

Country	Objectives
Australia	To raise, manage and retire Commonwealth debt at the lowest possible long-term cost, consistent with an acceptable degree of risk exposure.
Belgium	To minimize the financial cost of the debt with reference to the benchmark within pre-established risk limits.
Brazil	To reduce the maturity concentration; to optimize the external debt's average life; to reduce the cost of borrowing; to gradually substitute external restructured debt; to establish benchmark issues to amplify the investor base; to open the markets to other private and public borrowers.
Canada	To provide stable, low-cost funding for the government; and maintain and enhance a well-functioning market for Government of Canada securities.
Colombia	To minimize long term cost, respecting risk tolerance, while promoting an acceptable risk-return trade-off. An important objective is also to help develop the local market.
Denmark	To ensure low costs, with due consideration of the risk entailed by the government debt.
Finland	To minimize the effective cost of the debt, while not exceeding appropriate risk levels.
Ireland	To fund maturing debt, and manage the existing stock of debt in such a way as to protect both short-term and long-term liquidity, contain the level and volatility of annual fiscal debt service costs, and outperform a benchmark or shadow portfolio.
Italy	To minimize the projected cost of debt and to achieve a structural reduction of risk.
Mexico	To maintain a light external debt amortization profile, and to try to reduce costs while limiting refinancing risk.
The Netherlands	To fund the national debt in the most efficient manner possible, viewed over the longer term. This means minimizing the financing cost, commensurate with an acceptable level of risk.
New Zealand	Maximize the long-term economic return on the government's financial assets and debt in the context of the government's fiscal strategy, particularly its aversion to risk.
Portugal	To fulfill the borrowing requirements of the Republic in a stable manner and to minimize the cost of the government debt on a long-term perspective subject to the risk strategies defined by the Government.

Table 2: (continued)

Country	Objectives
Republic of Korea	To cover the Government's funding needs and minimizing debt service costs in the medium to long term and to foster the domestic bond market.
Sweden	To minimize the cost of borrowing, both over the long and the short term, within the existing framework and risk limits of its operations.
Thailand	To lower cost of borrowing; to manage refunding risk; to manage government's financing needs; and to promote local debt market.
United Kingdom	To carry out the Government's debt management policy of minimizing the financing cost over the long term taking account of risk, and to manage the aggregate cash needs of the Exchequer in the most cost-effective way.
United States	To borrow what is necessary to meet the monetary needs of the Government and to minimize the cost of borrowing to the Federal Government.

Source: Various debt office web sites and The World Bank.

weakness and, in some cases, in inability to access foreign capital markets. What may appear to be a cheaper transaction often entails significant risks for the government and constrains its capacity to repay lenders.

Cost and *market risk* are terms that are often used loosely by debt management practitioners. Their meaning is explored in chapter 4. Briefly, cost generally refers to the expected stream of cash flows associated with servicing (including repayment of principal) a series of debt obligations. The term can also be used to denote change in the market value of outstanding debt. Market risk—often referred to as *volatility*—measures the degree to which the cash flows associated with the stream of debt-servicing costs (or the market value of the debt) could change over time as a result of changes in interest rates, including country risk premia, in exchange rates, and in other market prices.

Avoiding sovereign debt default is usually an important objective of debt management in all countries, given the magnitude of the output losses and the human costs that can accompany default.[11] Business and banking insolvencies, and human distress and high unemployment, can result as access to foreign savings is reduced or closed off and the quality of bank portfolios deteriorate, precipitating a credit crunch.

The risk of default is especially relevant for countries that are heavily dependent on foreign currency and short-maturity borrowing. For many emerging market borrowers, the main debt management objective is to obtain financing at a reasonable cost; less attention is paid to managing market risk. When domestic capital markets are underdeveloped, domestic budgetary expenditures and infrastructure projects may need to be financed by debt denominated in or indexed to foreign currencies. This increases the government's foreign exchange risk if the cash flows available for servicing the debt are denominated in domestic currency and are not sensitive to exchange rate movements. When the government guarantees the foreign currency borrowing of subnational entities such as state governments and state-owned enterprises, its credit exposure can increase markedly if the funding creates currency mismatches on the borrower's balance sheet.

Failure to establish clear objectives for managing the costs and risks in its debt portfolio can be costly for a government. It can lead to uncertainty among government debt managers as to how to develop a strategy for managing the existing debt portfolio and to poor decisions on new borrowings. Lack of clear objectives, particularly on the risk management side, can result in an unmanaged buildup of contingent liabilities if decisionmakers seek to extend guarantees and other underwriting commitments as an alternative to direct financing. This can lead to large unrecorded claims on government assets and to further borrowing if the contingencies are drawn down at a later stage. As will be discussed in chapter 6, in some Asian economies in recent years, the realization of contingent liabilities in the banking sector has more than doubled the ratio of government debt to GDP.

Unclear debt management objectives also create uncertainty within the financial community. Investors incur costs in attempting to monitor and interpret the government's objectives and policy framework, and this uncertainty premium is quickly reflected in reduced demand for the government's securities, or in higher debt-servicing costs, or both.

Governments' cost and risk preferences change over time as policy priorities alter and capital market constraints ease. In general, the emphasis on risk reduction should be greater when the government's debt portfolio is large in relation to the economy's output and includes considerable foreign currency exposure and short-term debt. Countries that have less capacity to manage market risk and that need to borrow in foreign currencies should maintain lower debt levels than countries that can borrow extensively in their domestic currencies. For the first group, minimizing cost should not be the key focus of debt management. Instead, the main emphasis should be on reducing refinancing risk and market risk. Over time, if the government's balance sheet risks ease, the government may be able to assign greater weight to reducing expected debt-servicing costs.

DESIGNING A DEBT MANAGEMENT STRATEGY

In designing a debt management strategy, government debt managers are faced with several choices as to the financial characteristics of the debt. Among them are the following:

- The desired currency composition of the debt portfolio, including the mix between domestic currency debt and foreign currency debt

- The desired maturity structure and liquidity of the debt

- The appropriate duration or interest rate sensitivity of the debt

- Whether domestic currency debt should be in nominal terms or should be indexed to inflation or to a particular reference price

- Whether the portfolio composition should be transformed through swaps and other hedges, buybacks, or through new issuance.

Many of these decisions involve difficult tradeoffs. For example, foreign currency debt may be seen ex ante as cheaper than domestic currency debt of the same maturity, since the latter often involves a higher country risk and liquidity premium—perhaps because of inflation and political risk considerations or because the domestic market may be in its infancy. But foreign currency debt exposes the government's balance sheet to currency risk, whereas development of domestic debt markets can help reduce the government's overall balance sheet risk, promote diversification of the investor base, and, on an ex post basis, may result in lower borrowing costs. Foreign currency debt has in many situations proved to be expensive, especially when domestic economic policies and market conditions have caused the exchange rate to depreciate markedly.

Similarly, if there is a high inflation risk premium (or default risk premium) built into longer-term rates, short-term debt would, ex ante, be expected to be cheaper than long-term debt. Excessive short-term debt, however, increases risk by increasing the volatility of debt-servicing costs. Because short-term debt requires more frequent refinancing, there is always the risk that a government may be unable to access markets or will be able to do so only at very high spreads. Many sovereign defaults originate from situations of excessive short-term debt. Building up liquidity in longer-benchmark maturities can help reduce refinancing risk and decrease risk premia over time, even if there are higher debt-servicing costs when this strategy is initially adopted.

CHOICES RELATING TO TRANSACTION DECISIONS

Transaction-related decisions may involve, for example, forecasting the government's borrowing requirements and implementing its borrowing program; managing the government's cash balances to minimize carrying costs; undertaking transactions to move the portfolio composition of the debt closer to strategic benchmarks; and executing transactions of a tactical nature.

In making borrowing decisions, the debt manager faces such choices as:

- Whether to borrow from official sources (e.g., bilateral sources and international financial institutions) or from commercial creditors.

- Whether to borrow in the offshore capital market or in the syndicated bank loan market. Borrowers also need to decide the size and timing of their borrowing. Spreading out the borrowing enables borrowers to sample market conditions and possibly develop greater name recognition in the market. Concentrating borrowing in a smaller number of issues enables borrowers to meet their financing targets more quickly and creates larger, more liquid, benchmark issues.

- Whether to use derivatives in borrowing (e.g., whether to borrow through "plain vanilla" capital market instruments or through more structured transactions involving private placements), and, if derivatives are used, how to manage the ensuing counterparty credit risk.

Government debt managers also have to make a number of important portfolio management decisions, such as:

- Whether portfolio management transactions should always aim to move the actual portfolio closer to strategic benchmarks, or whether portfolio managers should be able to manage tactical positions in order to build up greater market knowledge at the risk of not generating acceptable risk-adjusted returns.

- How to establish position and loss limits if tactical trading is permitted.

- What mechanism to use to sell the debt (e.g., private placement, development of a tap mechanism, auction of the debt, or use of underwriters or primary dealers), and what institutional arrangements should be developed (the type of auction technique to be used, who is to conduct the auctions, what criteria should guide tap sales, whether primary dealers should be introduced, and, if they are, what process to use to appoint the dealers and how best to evaluate their performance).

- When to borrow—for example whether to issue domestic currency debt opportunistically or regularly and, if regularly, whether to base issuance on a preannounced calendar. In the case of foreign currency debt, debt managers need to decide how far in advance of the maturity of the existing debt obligation new borrowing should take place; that is, how much foreign currency liquidity the debt manager should be responsible for handling.

- Which markets the government should seek to borrow in and what types of transaction should be employed—e.g., whether the government should attempt to issue a global bond, access the euro market, target a particular country's institutional or retail sector, or issue a structured bond that meets the risk and return preferences of individual investors.

- What pricing strategy to adopt in launching a foreign currency issue and the criteria to be used in selecting the banks that will lead-manage the issue.

- What benchmark issues should be established and how much liquidity should be built up in each benchmark issue.

- Whether the government should seek to buy back its debt in the market and, if it does, at what price; what type of offer mechanism should be used; and whether the transaction should be a once-only action or part of a broader buyback program.

- What type of financial restructuring is required in order to strengthen the balance sheets of state-owned enterprises in financial difficulty.

ISSUES IN MANAGEMENT OF PUBLIC DEBT: AN OUTLINE

Sound government debt management requires analysis of fundamental public policy issues concerning the role and positioning of governments in financial markets and the interface of debt management and other economic policies. It involves consideration of the most appropriate use of the government's balance sheet, as well as technical analysis and judgment in managing the costs and risks associated with what are often very large and complex debt portfolios. For these reasons, government debt management is a specialized business within the public sector. Good debt management can avoid the common pitfalls described in box 1, above. Subsequent chapters explore in detail the elements of sound debt management and the issues surrounding it.

Chapter 2 discusses the interdependence between government debt management policy and other macroeconomic policy instruments. It examines the tensions that can arise among policymakers and how these can be lessened through institutional design, including more efficient contracting procedures.

In considering how best to build capacity in debt management, a critical step is to establish a set of governance practices embodying a solid legal foundation and sound risk management practices. Important considerations in designing a prudent governance framework are discussed in chapter 3, which also examines the types of agency cost that can arise when goals, accountabilities, and incentive structures are misaligned.

Developing clear strategic goals for debt management is essential. Chapter 4 presents a broad conceptual government balance sheet framework for anchoring a government debt management strategy. The framework offers rich insights for considering the preferred risk characteristics of a government debt portfolio and for analyzing a government's ownership interests in various businesses and deciding how best to manage them.

Risk management lies at the heart of government debt management. The various stages of the risk management process, and the types of policies adopted to manage risk are discussed in chapter 5.

Contingent liabilities often represent some of the largest risks in a government's balance sheet. These potential financial claims against the government can result in material financial obligations. They often are triggered during a banking crisis or at times when the economy, and therefore the government's fiscal flows, are under stress. Chapter 6 discusses the risks associated with these types of contingent liability and the role that government debt managers can play in mitigating them.

Strategic benchmarks are an essential element of portfolio and risk management. A strategic benchmark identifies a government's preferred cost-risk tradeoff on the basis of its tolerance for risk and its desire to reduce expected debt-servicing costs. Strategic benchmarks can be used to guide portfolio decisions (on types of borrowing instruments and on the currency composition, interest rate basis, and maturity of new borrowings) and to assess portfolio performance. Chapter 7 examines the characteristics of well-designed strategic benchmarks and how debt managers can best use them.

Efficient management information systems are crucial for asset and liability management. Government debt managers inevitably spend considerable time on systems issues as they strive to improve the quality of analysis and output. But systems investment decisions and implementation are areas in which costly mistakes can easily be made. Chapter 8 looks at the types of systems functionality needed in a debt office, describes the characteristics of good debt management systems, and explores a wide range of issues concerning management of the investment in information systems.

An important objective of government debt management, especially in emerging market countries, is to assist the development of efficient domestic money markets and fixed-income markets. Issuance of domestic currency bonds usually enables governments to reduce their balance sheet risk, smooth out their adjustment to adverse budgetary shocks, and diversify their funding sources. Especially in the case of emerging markets, it allows governments to reduce their dependence on foreign currency borrowing, access to which can dry up in situations of regional or global financial market contagion or when domestic policy imbalances cause the country's risk premium to rise rapidly. Government bond markets generate valuable externalities for the private sector by serving as a pricing benchmark for private sector contracting and assisting the development of derivatives markets. They also provide investors with an almost credit-risk-free asset when the government has a AAA credit rating in its domestic currency. Policy advisers, however, often face difficult decisions in developing these markets, as reviewed in chapter 9.

Finally, chapter 10 discusses important challenges involved in building capacity in government debt management.

NOTES

1. In Sweden the Debt Office of the Four Estates was founded in 1719 to manage the debt incurred in the wars of King Charles XII. In April 1789 the Swedish National Debt Office was established to manage the central government's debt. For a description of changes in the ratio of national

debt to gross national product (GNP) in the United Kingdom during the period 1688–1997, see Goodhart (1998).

2. This was especially the case with Belgium, Ireland, and New Zealand. In Finland and Sweden, deteriorating fiscal positions and rapidly expanding borrowing needs were important factors behind the upgrading of government debt management.

3. Governments often found that in order to implement medium-term financial strategies that were designed to achieve low and stable rates of inflation and reduce ratios of net public sector debt to GDP, comprehensive reforms in factor and product markets were necessary. Early adjustment efforts were often concentrated on financial sector deregulation and included review of capital controls, tax reform, labor market reform, social security and pension reform, and (sometimes) reductions in border protection.

4. During the 1990s, governments frequently sent missions to review the debt management approaches adopted by Belgium, Denmark, Ireland, New Zealand, and Sweden. International conferences and forums organized by the International Monetary Fund (IMF), the OECD, and the World Bank were also important—in particular, meetings of the Government Borrowers Forum and the Sovereign Debt Management Forum hosted by the World Bank and meetings of the OECD Debt Management Working Group. Technical assistance extended by these organizations, by the United Nations Conference on Trade and Development (UNCTAD), by the Commonwealth Secretariat, and by regional organizations such as the Macroeconomic and Financial Management Institute of Eastern and Southern Africa (MEFMI) has been influential in raising awareness of the need for capacity building in government debt management.

5. For example, the General Directorate of Public Credit in Colombia, the Asset and Liability Management Branch in South Africa's Department of Finance, and the Asset and Liability Management Branch in the New Zealand Treasury Department monitor explicit contingent liabilities as part of their responsibilities. The Swedish National Debt Office is responsible for assessing and valuing the risks associated with the issuance of government guarantees and for developing appropriate pricing policies.

6. A government balance sheet framework is a conceptual structure for considering the risk characteristics of a government's main asset and liability portfolios with a view to helping reduce the government's overall risk.

7. Fiscal decentralization is the process of devolving responsibility for the management of publicly provided goods and services from the central

government to other (e.g., state and local) levels of government or to public entities such as state-owned enterprises.

8. Some Eastern and Central European governments have adopted cautious borrowing policies. Nevertheless, their exposure to contingent liabilities (which represent potential claims against the government that can be triggered in certain situations) is often very large.

9. Sometimes corporate bodies, such as oil companies and important commodity producers, have a higher credit rating than the government, but usually the government has the highest credit rating, given its scope (at least in principle) to raise taxes and to draw on other sources of revenue to service debt obligations.

10. Prime bank note frauds come in many forms. In a common variation, a government or an investor is invited to purchase supposedly AAA-rated paper, which is said to bear extremely high financial returns (typically, several hundred percent annually) because it is portrayed as being subsidized by the U.S. Treasury, the World Bank, or the IMF as part of a covert arrangement to finance structural adjustment reform in certain developing countries.

11. Default may refer to the failure to repay foreign currency debt, which is usually held by external creditors. In a domestic market context, default can also refer to the erosion of bondholders' real wealth through inflation shocks, taxation, unanticipated regulation, and the unilateral extension of repayment terms.

Managing the Interface Between Debt Management Policy and Other Macroeconomic Policies

To help manage the government's balance sheet risk and reduce the economy's vulnerability to economic and financial shocks, government debt managers, fiscal policy advisers, and central bankers need a shared understanding of the objectives of debt management policy and of traditional macroeconomic policy instruments. Given the interdependencies between debt management policy, fiscal policy, and monetary policy, it is essential that they understand how the policy instruments operate, how they can reinforce one another, and how policy tensions can arise. This chapter discusses the nature of these interactions and the role that institutional design, contracting arrangements, and information sharing can play in supporting asset and liability management practices and in resolving policy differences between debt management policy and other macroeconomic policies. The assignment of policy instruments to well-defined policy objectives and the existence of supportive institutional arrangements are more evident in developed than in developing countries. The chapter therefore specifically discusses the complexities involved in the interaction of monetary policy and government debt management policy in many developing countries.

DEBT MANAGEMENT POLICIES, ECONOMIC POLICY SETTINGS, AND BANKING CRISES

Traditionally, most of the growth in net government indebtedness in the larger OECD countries has come from the cumulative impact of budget deficits (Chouraqui, Jones, and Montador 1986). In many emerging markets, however, an important source of growth in net government debt over the past 15 years has been a buildup in liabilities associated with recapitalizing public sector enterprises and restructuring the banking sector (see, for example, Kharas and Mishra 2001). Poor government debt management policies have also contributed to this growth. Fiscal policy practitioners use a number of measures to help assess the significance of the level and trend of public sector indebtedness and the vulnerability of the economy to exogenous shocks.[1] In making the assessments, several indicators are usually examined, as an isolated indicator can create a misleading impression. For example, several Latin American countries have moderate ratios of net public sector debt to GDP, but debt-servicing costs are high in relation to government tax revenue because inefficiently designed tax systems limit taxable capacity.[2]

Whatever their causes, large volumes of public debt and deteriorating fiscal positions can raise macroeconomic policy concerns by creating widespread uncertainty as to the sustainability of government expenditure and revenue trends and even the potential solvency of the government. These sentiments may be reflected in exchange rate weakness, increased country risk premia, and, in extreme cases, reluctance of domestic and foreign savers to lend to the government.

High and rapidly growing levels of public sector indebtedness affect private sector behavior by, for example, increasing the private sector's inflationary expectations and the pressure on monetary authorities to tighten monetary policy, especially if financial markets believe that the government lacks the commitment to restrain growth in its spending or to raise additional revenue. High real domestic interest rates and such measures as quantitative credit controls can crowd out the private sector from domestic financial markets, causing private sector borrowers to involuntarily take on higher foreign currency exposure. These crowding-out effects are likely to be more severe when the domestic capital market is less developed.

External financing can reduce these crowding-out effects by increasing borrowers' access to foreigners' savings. If, however, the external borrowing is in foreign currency (that is, if the borrower is unable to attract foreign savings by issuing debt in domestic currency), it creates currency risk, and the crowding-out effects are simply delayed until the foreign currency debt is serviced. If foreigners subsequently reinvest in the government's domestic currency securities, the crowding-out effects are delayed until the investor remits the repayments offshore. Many OECD governments can access foreign savings and eliminate currency risk by issuing securities in domestic currency, but few emerging market borrowers are able to attract substantial foreign savings by issuing bonds in their domestic currencies.

Prolonged fiscal deficits, and the increased real interest rates that accompany them, lead to slower growth in the capital stock and, potentially, a lower rate of output growth. Real wages decline as the marginal product of labor decreases (because labor has less capital with which to work). National income growth also slows as foreign investors increase their share of the returns on domestic assets. Higher levels of public debt therefore heighten an economy's vulnerability to economic and financial shocks, alter the distribution of factor income, and reduce policymakers' ability to manage the fiscal policy demands stemming from structural changes such as the additional income transfers and medical expenditures associated with an aging population.[3]

High and rising debt levels also have important fiscal effects through the generation of negative debt-servicing dynamics that exacerbate the government's fiscal position. In an adverse debt-servicing spiral, government debt-servicing costs increase rapidly as a share of overall government spending or of government revenue, and the government has to run larger primary surpluses to reduce its overall budget deficit.[4] This unfavorable debt-servicing arithmetic reflects the compounding effects of large government borrowing and increased country risk premia in the term structure.[5] These effects, in conjunction with the potential slowing of output growth and increased vulnerability, reduce the quality of the government's balance sheet and diminish the government's net worth. They also increase the likelihood of greater variability in future tax rates and create additional uncertainty for businesses and individuals with regard to spending decisions, thereby raising the option value of deferring investment decisions.[6]

Rapidly deteriorating public sector debt ratios, and the factors responsible for them, often lead to exchange rate pressures. Fears about possible future monetization of the debt can spur heavy capital outflows and can force policy makers to face difficult decisions about whether and by how much to tighten fiscal policy and monetary policy in order to defend a particular exchange rate level or band. Currency crises can quickly develop into banking crises, particularly if the credit squeeze, high real interest rates, and exchange rate depreciation increase insolvencies in a highly leveraged corporate and financial sector, where firms may have large, unhedged currency exposures. Fiscal pressures intensify and government borrowing increases as the slowdown in economic activity reduces tax revenue and the government faces potential financing demands to recapitalize parts of the banking system and state-owned enterprises or to finance government contingent liabilities that are falling due. As demonstrated by developments in Thailand in 1997, government contingent liabilities associated with banking sector bailouts can become extremely large when the banking sector's expectations of a continued fixed exchange rate policy encourages intermediaries to take large currency mismatches onto their balance sheets in search of higher returns—for example, by borrowing in short maturities in U.S. dollars and lending or investing in long-maturity local currency assets (Cooper 1999).

Sound monetary and fiscal policies and high domestic savings rates may not, however, be sufficient to protect an economy from a financial crisis, as illustrated by the Asian economic crisis in the late 1990s. Adverse terms of trade shocks, poor asset and liability management practices in the private sector, and the balance sheet exposures of the banking sector, with their implications for possible future government capital injections, can all increase the risk of crisis. So, too, can inappropriate government debt management.

This is especially so when a government's debt portfolio contains substantial amounts of short-term debt or large holdings of debt denominated in, or indexed to, foreign currency. High borrowing needs (and the expectation that these needs would persist) and the large refinancing risk posed by short-term local currency debt were key factors behind the Russian government's default in August 1998. Concerns about the magnitude of the appreciation in Mexico's real exchange rate, the size of the current account deficit, and declining international reserves—coupled with the short maturity of government borrowing and the extensive issuance of government short-term borrowing instruments (*tessabonos*) that were indexed to movements in the U.S. dollar exchange rate—lay behind the Mexican financial crisis of late 1994 and 1995 (Edwards 1999).

Given an increasingly interdependent global economy and greater capital account liberalization, contagion forces can intensify the cross-border transmission of financial crises. This can occur as a result of trade linkages, where currency devaluations in major trading partners force devaluations elsewhere, or through herding behavior among investors that results in strong capital outflows. Institutional investors, which increasingly dominate financial markets, herd into similar markets and instruments, taking the same types of position, and diverge only at the margin to beat short-term performance benchmarks that are shared by many. They have simultaneous access to the same information and use similar risk management technology. When one institution reaches its limits, others often do too. In times of stress, these investors sell their most volatile or highly correlated assets. When liquidity in some emerging market countries disappears, investors may endeavor to reduce their exposure to the general asset class by selling in other, more liquid, markets (White 2000).

Although prudent government debt management policies by themselves cannot prevent financial crises, they can be an important factor in supporting the macroeconomic policy framework and enhancing the credibility of economic management. Transparency in government debt management can highlight the need to improve macroeconomic policies. For example, an inability to implement an agreed debt management strategy due to changes in market conditions arising from slippages in macroeconomic policies can act as an early warning. In turn, sound macroeconomic policies are a precondition for high-quality government debt management. It is difficult to develop the latter when government indebtedness is increasing at an unsustainable rate and inappropriate macroeconomic and regulatory policies stifle the development of the domestic government securities market. In such circumstances, a government is often forced to incur substantial rollover risk because of excessive borrowing in short-term domestic instruments or to take foreign currency exposure onto its balance sheet.

The cost of financial sector crises can be very large. Box 2 illustrates the magnitude of the output losses associated with two financial crises in the 1990s: in Latin America (the "Tequila crisis") and in East Asia (the "East Asian crisis"). Table 3 summarizes the effect that the East Asian crisis of the late 1990s had on poverty levels in that region. The adjustment burden in East Asia fell disproportionately on the middle class and the poor and was reflected in an increase in poverty, reversing a three-decade-long trend of falling poverty in the region.

Banking crises have become much more frequent since 1973 than in the preceding 25 years because of the easing and removal of the tight regulations surrounding domestic and international capital markets (Bordo

Box 2
Cumulative output losses from financial crises in the 1990s

Shown in the table are estimates of the output losses associated with financial market crises during the 1990s. These losses resulted in Thailand's first
recession in 40 years and in Indonesia's and Korea's first recessions since
1965 and 1980, respectively.

	Cumulative four-year output losses (percent)[a]
"Tequila crisis" (1994–95)	
Argentina	15
Mexico	30
East Asian crisis (1997–98)	
Indonesia	73
Korea, Rep. of	14
Malaysia	34
Thailand	59

Note: The calculations for Thailand cover the period 1997–2000. For Indonesia, Korea, and
Malaysia, the estimates refer to the period 1998–2001.

a. Output losses are calculated as the sum of the output gap over a four-year period,
commencing with the year of the financial crisis. The output gap represents the percentage
difference between the actual level of real GDP and the potential level of GDP for each
country (i.e., the difference between actual and potential output). Potential output is defined
as the level of output consistent with the natural rate of unemployment and a "normal" rate
of capacity utilization.

Source: Unofficial IMF staff estimates.

and others 2001). The fiscal costs of addressing banking crises have been
enormous; a study by Honohan and Klingebiel (2003) found that these
costs averaged 12.8 percent of GDP in 40 country experiences over the
period 1970–2000. The costs for the developing countries represented in
the survey averaged 14.3 percent of GDP. Some banking sector overhauls
were even more expensive. The fiscal cost of the crises in Argentina and
Chile in the early 1980s was estimated to be 40–55 percent of GDP, and
some estimates of the fiscal costs of dealing with the banking sector problems in the countries most affected by the East Asian crisis in the late 1990s
are of a similar magnitude.

Table 3: Poverty in East Asia: 1987, 1996, and 1998
   (*millions of people*)

	1987	1996	1998	Attributable to crisis-induced poverty
Income of less than US$1 a day				
Total East Asia	418	265	278	13
East Asia 5[a]	114	55	65	10
China	304	210	213	3
Income of less than US$2 a day				
Total East Asia	1,052	864	892	28
East Asia 5[a]	300	236	260	24
China	752	628	632	4

a. Indonesia, Korea, Malaysia, Philippines, and Thailand.
Source: World Bank staff estimates contained in World Bank 2000a.

OPERATIONAL INTERDEPENDENCE AMONG DEBT MANAGEMENT POLICY, FISCAL POLICY, AND MONETARY POLICY

Fiscal policy advisers and government debt managers interact in several areas. Both share a common interest in ensuring that growth of public debt remains on a sustainable path and that a sound fiscal strategy is in place to reduce excessive levels of public sector debt.[7] Both are involved in developing objectives and a risk management framework for government debt management. The exact assignment of responsibilities depends on the broader governance arrangements for debt management. For example, if a debt office with operational responsibility for implementing debt management policy is established outside the ministry of finance, the ministry of finance should advise the government on debt management goals and important debt management policies or guidelines.[8]

Close coordination between the government's fiscal policy advisers and its debt managers is required in preparing the government's budget and other fiscal projections. As input into these projections, the government debt manager provides debt-servicing forecasts, which in turn depend on the finance ministry's economic forecasts and assumptions regarding future movements of interest and exchange rates and the primary balance. Government debt managers also provide advice on the size and composition of the government's borrowing program and on how it should be structured and amended as a result of new fiscal information, including changes in the government's projected cash position.

Considerable coordination is also required in daily cash management. Reliable forecasts of daily government departmental expenditure and revenue flows are needed in order to determine the size of the net liquidity flows between the government and the banking system. These forecasts enable the government's cash managers (that is, the government debt managers or the central bank acting as agent for the government debt managers) to identify the size of the injection or withdrawal of liquidity needed to neutralize these flows and help preserve the monetary policy framework, as discussed in "Government Cash Management," below.

In addition, government debt managers advise the government on possible market reaction to upcoming fiscal announcements and often provide advice on the operation of domestic capital markets and the financial management of the government's investment in state-owned enterprises. The issues might include restructuring the balance sheets of government-owned entities, privatizing state-owned enterprises, removing distortions impeding the efficiency of the domestic financial market, managing the government's relationship with the sovereign credit rating agencies, and advising how to manage the risks associated with contingent liabilities.[9] In some instances, the debt manager's advice may be required to help the central bank assess the significance of the private sector's foreign currency exposures.

Government debt managers' operational relationships with central banks can be complex. The central bank often provides a wide range of agency services for government debt managers. At the same time, the monetary authorities want to be sure that government debt management operations do not undermine their monetary policy and exchange rate management objectives. Government debt managers, for their part, will want to be certain that the cost and risk objectives for government debt management are not compromised in this relationship. (See the discussion in the next section.)

Many central banks provide registry and fiscal agency services for government debt managers by maintaining a register of owners of government securities and acting as paying agent for the government in the domestic market. Within the wholesale debt market, the central bank is frequently the debt manager's agent for undertaking liquidity management transactions through daily open market operations designed to neutralize the government's liquidity flows. (In some countries, including France, Ireland, Sweden, and the United Kingdom, these daily liquidity management operations are undertaken directly by the government debt managers.)

It is common for the central bank to conduct government bond and bill tenders or auctions for government debt managers. In addition, given the shared interest that the central bank and the debt managers have in developing an efficient domestic market, central banks often provide advice to the debt managers on debt management strategy and issuance decisions relating to the local market. This advice may cover topics such as the types of debt instrument to issue and their tax treatment; how to extend the yield curve; how much liquidity to target or commit to in establishing government benchmark securities; the selling techniques best suited for issuing in the market; and buyback or bond-switching opportunities. It is important that there be clarity as to who has the final decisionmaking authority in the event that the debt managers and the central bank disagree on these technical issues. In this situation, the decisionmaking authority for debt management operations should rest with the government debt managers.

In emerging market countries, government foreign currency borrowing is frequently carried out by the central bank on behalf of the ministry of finance. Because of the central banks' responsibilities for monetary policy and foreign exchange reserve management, they have greater numbers of staff with capital market experience and, often, better market-related systems technology than the finance ministry. In OECD countries, foreign currency borrowing by the central bank is much less common. Several OECD governments (such as the United States, Japan, and Germany) choose not to borrow in foreign currency at all and many, such as Denmark, Finland, Ireland, New Zealand, Norway, and Sweden significantly reduced their government foreign currency debt during the 1990s because of the currency risk it would bring to the government's balance sheet (refer to table 4).[10] In those OECD governments that continue to borrow foreign currency debt (often in order to refinance maturing foreign currency debt), the borrowing is nearly always carried out by the debt office.[11] In both OECD and emerging market countries, the government debt manager is often required to purchase from the central bank all of the foreign currency needed to service interest rate payments on the government's foreign currency debt.

Government debt managers need to have a sound understanding of the government's reasons for maintaining foreign exchange reserves and the central bank's objectives for managing the foreign currency investment and intervention portfolios comprising those reserves. This is especially relevant when the government's objective is to reduce risk on its balance sheet by ensuring that the foreign currency composition of part of its foreign currency debt matches the currency composition of the central bank's foreign exchange reserves. A clear understanding of the government's exchange rate objectives also helps in designing a foreign currency liability

Table 4: Percentage share of foreign currency denominated debt in total central government debt outstanding, 1990–2001, for selected OECD countries

Year	1990	1992	1994	1996	1998	2000	2001
Australia	27	12	6	2	1	1	1
Austria	15	16	19	19	24	12	12
Belgium	5	5	6	6	6	2	2
Canada	1	1	2	3	6	6	6
Denmark	23	18	19	14	12	12	12
Finland	39	61	52	40	32	15	15
France	n.a.	3	4	5	7	0	0
Ireland	n.a.	n.a	n.a	29	24	6	6
Iceland	50	54	52	56	51	60	65
Italy	5	5	7	7	6	4	3
Mexico	33	32	35	45	40	33	30
New Zealand	n.a.	43	37	25	22	22	22
Norway	10	24	22	15	3	3	2
Poland	n.a.	n.a.	13	13	9	8	8
Slovak Republic	n.a.	n.a.	n.a.	n.a.	21	39	22
Spain	2	3	2	2	3	4	4
Sweden	13	28	30	28	25	18	19
Turkey	2	2	5	10	7	8	9

Note: Total central government debt is the sum of total marketable and non-marketable debt issued by the central government. Data are based on national currency for the relevant fiscal year. Foreign currency debt is converted to domestic currency at end of year exchange rates. Financial derivatives are excluded.

Source: OECD National Accounts Statistics, Central Government Debt, Summary tables, Vol 2003, release 01.

benchmark and in advising the government as to the mix of domestic currency debt and foreign currency debt that might be appropriate.

Foreign currency reserves held by the central bank, along with any stand-by financing facilities (assuming that these remain available at all times), represent a substantial part of the foreign currency liquidity in the government's balance sheet. When the government debt managers are responsible for undertaking the government's foreign currency borrowing, they can advise the central bank on the least-cost way of obtaining a particular currency exposure for its reserves or of obtaining emergency financing, if needed. They can also help calculate the carrying costs associated with purchasing highly creditworthy but low-yielding foreign currency assets as part of the central bank's investment portfolio. These carrying costs, which reflect credit spread differentials, can be particularly large for emerging market borrowers.

POTENTIAL TENSIONS BETWEEN GOVERNMENT DEBT MANAGEMENT AND MACROECONOMIC POLICIES

Policy tensions can arise between government debt managers and other macroeconomic policy advisers when policy objectives and accountabilities for implementing debt management, and monetary and fiscal policies are not defined clearly enough. This situation creates the potential for damaging, opportunistic behavior, with the political and economic costs that were discussed in chapter 1. For example, a frequent practice in OECD countries in the 1970s, and one that persists in some emerging market countries, involves governments' pressuring or directing their debt managers to borrow in low-coupon foreign currencies in order to lower the recorded debt-servicing costs shown in the budget, regardless of the additional risk to the government's balance sheet. In a similar vein, members of the government are sometimes unwilling to disclose to their fiscal policy advisers and debt managers the contingent obligations (such as guarantees) or other off-balance-sheet commitments into which they have entered.

Some of the potential conflicts that develop between government debt management policy and macroeconomic policy have to do with time consistency and the credibility of macroeconomic policy. A policy setting is time inconsistent if it is viewed as creating an incentive for a government to reverse the policy for its own ends at a later time.[12] Public debt creates the potential for a government to adopt time-inconsistent strategies that reduce the government's debt-servicing costs, thereby lowering bondholders' returns. A government could, for example, issue long-dated fixed-rate nominal debt instruments and subsequently reduce bondholders' returns by generating surprise inflation (which, in real terms, is a form of default); by making unexpected changes in tax policy; or by defaulting on payment obligations. This strategy can be costly because of the economic distortions created by high and variable rates of inflation, the subsequent output losses in disinflating, and the fact that bondholders will be reluctant to provide additional financing in the future or will only do so at interest rates that compensate them adequately for the additional risks.[13] Investors recognize that the government could endeavor to reduce the value of its liabilities through inflation or through tax or interest rate adjustments and will price these concerns into their bids for government securities. In addition, investors may seek instruments or arrangements that make it more costly or more difficult for the government to default, or instruments that assign investors a higher standing in the event of default. Often, these proposals may appear inexpensive to the government (as might any option embedded in a contingent claim), but they can carry high risks.

Most governments seek to avoid issuing a mix of debt instruments with differing creditor rights, in order to prevent hostile creditors from leveraging such influence and involving the issuer in expensive litigation in the event of full or partial default. Governments in developed countries, for example, generally seek to limit their issuance to one or two types of debt instrument, with a range of maturities but without creating different seniorities among creditor classes. The challenge for government debt managers is to provide a debt structure that reduces the risks of the government's defaulting but also avoids excessive negotiation costs in the event that the government is, for any reason, forced to default (see Dooley 2000).

Conflicts between the central bank and government debt managers can arise if the central bank believes that the key role of debt management policy should be to reinforce the government's or the central bank's commitment to low inflation and thereby help lower inflationary expectations. To reduce the time-inconsistent incentives facing the government and to strengthen the signaling role of monetary policy, proponents of this view suggest that the government increase the proportion of foreign currency debt or debt linked to a foreign currency index in its debt portfolio; issue more floating-rate domestic currency debt; or introduce or issue more inflation-indexed debt. Under each issuance strategy, the government is perceived to have little incentive to generate surprise inflation because that would feed back quickly into higher debt-servicing costs through a lower exchange rate or a higher interest rate. With foreign currency debt, the government, rather than the bondholder, would bear the risk of an inflation-induced exchange rate depreciation. Similarly, more floating-rate debt would mean that the government would incur the risk of any increase in interest rates. By issuing inflation-indexed debt, the government, according to this argument, would be indicating its willingness to compensate bondholders for inflation and, by implication, would be signaling that it has an incentive to achieve low and stable rates of inflation. A contrary view is that issuing inflation-indexed debt would indicate that the government is willing to support the concept of an indexed economy, thereby increasing inflationary expectations among wage and price setters.

Government debt managers, for their part, may believe that shortening portfolio duration and taking on more foreign currency exposure would increase the riskiness of the government's debt portfolio and its balance sheet and undermine its debt management framework. They often prefer to concentrate their domestic issuance on longer-maturity fixed-rate instruments in order to help reduce refinancing risks, stabilize debt-servicing costs, increase the investor base and the depth of the domestic bond market, and establish a pricing benchmark to help the market in pricing the credit of other domestic fixed-income issuers. (Table 5 illustrates how several OECD countries have increased the proportion of fixed rate debt in their total outstanding central government debt during the 1990s.) They may believe that domestic investors, who are usually the predominant purchasers of inflation-indexed debt instruments, are not adequately prepared for the introduction of these instruments. For example, investors might not sufficiently understand the risk and return characteristics of the instrument or the nature of the liquidity premium, or a separate asset allocation class may not have been established in the pension investment industry at that stage. This situation would create risks of poor investor coverage in auctions, low prices, and insufficient liquidity, all of which would damage the reputation of the government debt managers.

Sometimes these policy tensions can be more subtle. For example, the central bank may believe that in order to improve its market intelligence and increase its readiness to undertake foreign currency intervention, its foreign exchange dealers should have a monopoly on the purchase of foreign currency needed by the debt office to service the government's foreign currency debt. Alternatively, government debt managers may believe that the central bank dealers are unable to provide competitive foreign exchange quotes because they are not sufficiently active in the market and do not see enough of the transaction flows to readily offset their positions with major domestic sellers of foreign currency such as large exporters. Government debt managers (and some central bank staff) may also be concerned that markets will not be able to distinguish between foreign currency purchases transacted as part of debt-servicing obligations on foreign currency borrowings and a currency intervention undertaken as part of exchange rate management. These issues can result in a blurring of the roles and responsibilities of central bankers and government debt managers.

In some situations, debt management decisions can reinforce the signaling effects of monetary policy. This could occur, for example, when debt managers want to issue inflation-indexed debt or foreign currency debt in order to diversify the investor base and reduce refinancing risk. But these

Table 5: Percentage share of fixed-rate long-term debt in total central government debt outstanding, 1990–2001, in selected OECD countries

Time period	1990	1992	1994	1996	1998	2000	2001
Australia	53	61	69	70	72	75	77
Austria	53	58	64	67	75	81	85
Belgium	51	61	59	69	72	74	78
Canada	32	32	36	40	42	44	41
Czech Republic	n.a.	n.a.	14	21	26	27	39
Denmark	59	61	68	78	82	77	74
Germany	75	83	85	80	84	85	87
Finland	42	69	65	61	77	66	63
France	n.a.	66	74	75	76	79	77
Greece	n.a.	n.a.	2	1	22	43	54
Hungary	2	7	6	6	14	27	34
Iceland	26	32	38	38	36	29	28
Italy	20	25	38	39	44	52	54
Japan	64	62	59	58	59	57	59
Korea	35	43	51	66	60	71	78
Luxembourg	83	83	92	96	93	94	86
Mexico	23	21	23	29	32	32	37
Netherlands	65	72	76	82	79	84	80
New Zealand	n.a.	58	56	54	58	60	61
Norway	43	49	59	46	48	43	39
Poland	n.a.	n.a.	9	14	18	37	43
Portugal	1	8	18	25	38	66	68
Slovak Republic	n.a.	n.a.	16	45	73	81	67
Spain	28	39	52	57	71	79	84
Sweden	49	60	64	67	69	64	63
Switzerland	30	33	37	38	40	50	58
United States	54	55	57	56	55	51	47
United Kingdom	38	40	33	31	34	29	31

Note: Total central government debt is the sum of total marketable and non-marketable debt issued by the central government. Fixed rate instruments include medium and long term bonds; they exclude short term debt up to 1 year to maturity. Data are based on national currency for the relevant fiscal year. Financial derivatives are excluded.

Source: OECD National Accounts Statistics, Central Government Debt, Summary tables, Vol 2003, release 01.

debt management instruments should not be adopted for signaling reasons if they compromise the government's debt management strategy by bringing excessive risk onto the government's balance sheet. Other policy initiatives are better suited for enhancing the credibility of monetary policy. Among them are increasing the independence of the central bank, adopting supportive fiscal policies, deregulating the labor market, and introducing other positive adjustment policies such as lowering the levels of border protection and removing regulatory barriers in the sheltered or nontradables sector in order to enhance productivity and competitiveness.

GOVERNMENT CASH MANAGEMENT

Because of its multiple dimensions, the term "government cash management" is often used loosely by policymakers, and governments have taken a variety of approaches in deciding where these management responsibilities should rest. In general, government cash management tends to have two objectives. The first is to ensure that government departments and agencies manage their cash balances efficiently so that the government does not have "surplus" cash on hand (which would mean that debt managers had borrowed excessively in capital markets and thereby incurred unnecessary debt-servicing costs and additional risk for the government). The second objective is to neutralize the impact on the domestic banking sector of the government's cash flows, which arise from government spending and revenue collection and from investment in and divestment of government assets. This neutralization is necessary to ensure that government transactions do not create large and unpredictable changes in liquidity in the banking system and undermine monetary policy.

At the heart of government cash management is an efficient government accounting system and sound procedures for monitoring and controlling government spending and for forecasting revenues. Developing and maintaining these systems is usually a core responsibility of the ministry of finance.

To build a sound foundation for government financial management, budgetary analysis, and responsible cash management, government agencies have to forecast their revenue and spending flows regularly. For budgetary analysis, this information may be needed monthly or more frequently. Government cash managers in developed government debt markets, however, require daily forecasts in order to assess the size of the offsetting market transactions needed to neutralize the government's net cash injections into or withdrawal from the domestic banking system as a result of its daily operations.[14] Government departments and ministries may be required to forecast, at the beginning of the year, their monthly, weekly, and daily spending and revenue patterns for the year and to update them constantly during the year. Comparison between these forecasts and actual departmental revenue and spending patterns provides valuable insight into how the principal government spending agencies are managing their cash flows.

It is not necessary for government debt managers to be involved in collecting the forecasts of departmental revenue and expenditure, although the debt office might undertake cash flow modeling on the basis of past flows in order to check the consistency of fiscal flows. Detailed cash flow data are usually collected in the ministry of finance (e.g., in a budget or a financial management department). It is essential that government debt managers have access both to these forecasts and to comparisons with actual cash balances so that they can gauge the size of the required liquidity management transactions, assess the quality of cash management in government agencies, and review and if necessary amend the government's overall borrowing program. If the central bank undertakes the liquidity management transactions as an agent for the government debt managers, it will require this information as well, although it could also project liquidity flows on the basis of historical patterns and by obtaining forecasts from the larger government agencies.[15]

Measures should be considered to encourage heads of government departments to take cash management seriously by improving the efficiency of their working capital cycles and reducing their daily cash balances. Sound practices include collecting revenues and other receivables quickly; developing policies for procurement and negotiating payment cycles with creditors in order to secure the best pricing and payment terms; and taking measures to rationalize the opening and use of departmental bank accounts and to ensure that revenues are deposited quickly. Sanctions and incentives to promote efficient departmental cash management can play an important role because heads of government departments are funded centrally and otherwise would not usually bear the cost of their funding or the consequences of poor cash management. Sanctions could include reduced levels of funding or the payment of interest on the excess cash balances to the ministry of finance. Government debt managers should be consulted in designing any system of sanctions and incentives. They should also be involved in considering issues such as whether government departments should be free to manage their own banking relationships, and whether there is merit in tendering out government departments' day-to-day banking business to one or more commercial banks with the aim of obtaining lower fees and a wider range of banking services.

Whenever possible, governments should seek to separate cash or liquidity management transactions from the implementation of monetary policy. When the central bank is undertaking liquidity management transactions on behalf of government debt managers, the debt managers will require that the size of the daily open market operations (or whatever instrument is used to manage government liquidity) match or closely approximate the forecast liquidity injection or withdrawal. For example, treasury bills might be used by the central bank to undertake open market operations for liquidity management purposes on behalf of government debt managers. If there is a substantial net cash injection from the government to the banking sector on a particular day (e.g., because of pension payments), the central bank could offset it by using repo or selling treasury bills to the commercial banks for the amount of the forecast net injection. Or, if there is a substantial drain from the banking system to the government—say, because of tax payments—the central bank could inject liquidity into the banking system by using reverse repo or buying treasury bills equivalent to the amount of the expected net withdrawal of liquidity.

Although debt managers may be prepared to reject bids that are uncompetitive, they would not wish to see the central bank alter the size of its daily open market operations with a view to signaling a change in monetary policy. If the central bank announced much larger open market operations than needed for the government's liquidity management purposes and this involved selling treasury bills or similar instruments, financial markets would view this move as indicating a desire by the central bank for tighter monetary conditions or a firmer monetary policy. Similarly, where government debt managers undertake their own cash management transactions, the central bank will want to see that the daily liquidity transactions undertaken do not differ materially from the liquidity target. Such a difference could cause the financial markets to question the credibility of monetary policy or to assume that the government debt managers' excess trades represent a government interest rate view or signal a change in the government's budgetary position.

Addressing these agency costs through formal institutional arrangements such as agency agreements can be valuable in clarifying the respective responsibilities of the government debt managers and the central bank. These arrangements are discussed in the next section.

INSTITUTIONAL ARRANGEMENTS FOR ALLEVIATING TENSIONS BETWEEN DEBT MANAGEMENT POLICY AND MACROECONOMIC POLICIES

Potential policy conflicts among monetary, fiscal, and debt management policies can be alleviated by announcing clear goals for these policies and by maintaining a macroeconomic policy mix—particularly between monetary and fiscal policy—that is balanced, compatible with the existing exchange rate regime, and supportive of price stability and economic growth. Over the past decade, several governments have successfully established targets for key macroeconomic policy indicators in an endeavor to prevent major economic imbalances that would undermine growth prospects.[16] Some, such as Brazil and New Zealand, have introduced legislation requiring governments to manage their fiscal positions prudently and have announced criteria for assessing fiscal prudence. These measures have also involved the use of fiscal targets.[17]

It is particularly important to separate the accountability for debt management policy from that for monetary policy and to clarify the reporting, decisionmaking, and advisory responsibilities of the various institutions, given the very different objectives of monetary policy and debt management policy.[18] If accountability is not separated, debt management policy could be used as an instrument of monetary policy, aimed solely at reinforcing price stability objectives (e.g., by issuing excessive amounts of short-duration, indexed, or foreign currency debt). In such circumstances, debt management decisions would not be based on sound portfolio considerations, and the government's risk management framework would inevitably be compromised. There is also a danger that the reverse situation could occur, with central bankers facing political pressure to keep short-term interest rates low in an attempt by the government to stimulate private sector spending and contain government debt-servicing expenditures in the short run. Numerous country episodes illustrate both the unsustainable nature and the cost of these approaches (see, for example, OECD 1988).

In cases where the central bank plays a key operational role for government debt managers by providing registry and fiscal agency services or conducting regular auctions of government debt, many governments have sought to formalize these arrangements through an agency or service agreement between the debt office and the central bank. These agency agreements outline policy objectives and accountabilities and the structure of compensation for services, e.g., registry fees or charges for auctioning securities, and they incorporate quality and reporting standards in the same manner as if the debt managers were contracting services from private sector providers. Where the central bank undertakes daily cash management transactions for government debt managers, the agreement might, for example, contain language specifying that the open market operations cannot be used to signal a change in monetary policy. Such an agreement should clarify who decides the quantity and pricing of transactions and the criteria used to guide these decisions.

These types of agency agreements can help reduce market uncertainty as to the objectives and accountabilities associated with debt management policy and monetary policy. Agency agreements should be signed by the heads of the central bank and the debt office or by their representatives. As with any contractual relationship, government debt managers and central bank staff should regularly discuss operating issues that arise under the agency agreement and should exchange views on performance.

Where government debt managers undertake their own cash management transactions, agreement is needed to ensure that their operations do not undermine the central bank's monetary policy operations. Such an agreement could, for example, prohibit government debt managers from taking speculative positions based on interest rate decisions by the central bank or from intermediating between market participants for the purpose of grossing up the government's balance sheet.[19] As discussed in the next section, where capital markets are thin or underdeveloped, a clear separation between debt management policy and monetary policy is often not possible.

COORDINATING MONETARY POLICY AND DEBT MANAGEMENT POLICY DURING LIBERALIZATION OF FINANCIAL MARKETS

When domestic money markets and bond markets are well developed, the presence of a secondary market for government debt allows separation of the implementation of monetary policy and debt management. Under these conditions, the government can finance its domestic currency borrowing needs in the primary market by, for example, auctioning bonds to institutional bidders, while the central bank is able to influence monetary conditions and signal changes in monetary policy by buying and selling securities in the secondary market.

Separating debt management and monetary policy is much more difficult where government debt managers are funding their borrowing in the primary market and the central bank is seeking to implement monetary policy through similar channels. This interconnection between debt management policy and monetary policy is clearest when a government seeks to finance its budget deficit by borrowing from the central bank. This creates a direct link between the change in the fiscal deficit and the growth in the money supply. The government issues a government security or a promise to pay to the central bank in return for accessing overdraft facilities, and the recipients of the government payments, such as suppliers, welfare beneficiaries, and public servants, receive monetary assets in the form of cash or claims on bank reserves.

Where indirect instruments of monetary policy do not exist, the central bank usually endeavors to control the price or volume of private sector credit through direct interventions, such as credit and interest rate controls, and through directives that allocate credit to various sectors of the economy.[20] As other captive sources of control develop, emerging market governments can constrain credit growth by imposing limits on the size of the central bank overdraft facilities available to the government.

For a time, direct controls can enable a government to control the growth and pattern of lending. But therein lies the main weakness of direct instruments. Their ease of operation and their effectiveness in the short run can delay the development of institutional reforms that can promote more market based instruments and mechanisms for setting interest rates, and thereby for allocating credit. Direct forms of intervention in credit can eventually lead to significant allocative distortions: credit does not necessarily flow to the areas where it generates the highest economic returns, and managerial decisionmaking in financial intermediaries becomes heavily influenced by a desire to generate higher financial returns in less regulated sectors. This process can lead to significant financial market disintermediation, where credit increasingly flows from controlled to unregulated sectors in an endeavor to circumvent interest rate and credit controls.[21]

Cooperation and coordination between monetary and fiscal authorities are more important than ever in these situations. On the policy front, fiscal discipline is essential. Sizeable fiscal imbalances make it more difficult to reduce allocative distortions and financial sector disintermediation, given that the government's response may be to impose a wider range of controls on financial institutions, such as requiring them to purchase government securities at below-market interest rates. In order to avoid serious inflationary problems (and the inevitable economic and social costs, including increased poverty, that often accompany high and variable rates of inflation), it is essential that the ministry of finance share information with the central bank on the government's borrowing needs and the timing of government expenditure and revenue flows.

Central banks often face considerable difficulties in making the transition from direct to indirect instruments of monetary intervention: the treasury bill and government bond market may be fragile; a history of direct intervention has often resulted in a buildup of excessive liquidity; and cooperation and coordination between the central bank and the ministry of finance may be inadequate. In such circumstances, central banks often issue their own securities.

The central bank's issuance of securities should, whenever possible, be coordinated with that of the ministry of finance. Ideally, the central bank should seek to match the securities it issues with those issued by the ministry of finance or the debt management office (e.g., same maturity and same coupon structure) and to have parallel selling arrangements. Having such homogeneous products can enhance the overall depth of the money market. Often, however, such harmonization will not be feasible. Then, the central bank should seek to operate at the short end of the yield curve, while the ministry of finance concentrates its issuance on longer maturities. For these arrangements to succeed, the government must be willing to compensate the central bank for losses it incurs in buying and selling securities, with the aim of managing monetary conditions.

As the overall money and bond market develops, it should become possible for the central bank to conduct its operations by trading government securities in the secondary market. This would bring about important benefits: the central bank and the ministry of finance would no longer be competing for funds in the primary market; the bond and bill market would be less segmented; and the overall liquidity of that market would be increased.

In an emerging market context, it is all the more important that monetary authorities and government debt managers discuss their respective operational arrangements. To ensure that the instruments used for debt management and monetary policy do not undermine one another, coordination is needed to work out what instruments or forms of control will be used to finance the government's borrowing needs and how they will be applied. The latter considerations include the set of institutions covered, the frequency of use, and procedures for consultation when the instruments change.

Coordination can often be achieved through a committee of senior managers from the ministry of finance, the central bank, and possibly a planning ministry or the prime minister's department. These managers could meet to share information on large financial flows and discuss implementation issues. Below the committee level, considerable sharing of technical and fiscal information between the ministry of finance and the central bank is likely to be needed.

NOTES

1. Indicators typically used to assess the magnitude of the stock of government debt outstanding are the ratios of gross and net government debt to GDP and of annual government debt-servicing costs to total government spending or revenue. Often, these indicators are projected forward on the basis of assumptions about real GDP growth, future fiscal deficits, and changes in real interest rates and exchange rates.

A number of indicators used to assess external vulnerability are summarized in the IMF paper "Debt- and Reserve-Related Indicators of External Vulnerability" (IMF 2000), which pays particular attention to the relationship between the level of short-term (up to one year) public and private sector external debt and the size of the government's foreign exchange reserves. Examples of early-warning indicators used to help identify the roles of domestic and external factors in emerging market crises are given in Kamin, Schindler, and Samuel (2001).

2. During the 1980s, the ratio of the fiscal deficit to GDP averaged 6.3 percent for Latin American countries and 4.5 percent for OECD countries. Relative to government revenue, the consolidated central government fiscal deficits for these country groups were 32.5 and 17 percent, respectively. If the two largest economies in each group (Brazil and the United States) are excluded, total consolidated central government revenue as a share of GDP for the period 1970–94 was 15.5 percent in Latin America and 28 percent in OECD countries. See Gavin and others (1996).

3. Ball and Mankiw (1995) estimated that the long-term adverse impact of prolonged fiscal deficits (as opposed to continuous balanced budgets) in the United States was equivalent to between 3 and 6 percent of national income, or to having no growth in per capita income for a period of 1½ to 3 years.

4. In order to stabilize the government debt-to-GDP ratio when the nominal interest rate is higher than the nominal GDP growth rate, the primary budget balance has to be in surplus.

5. For a discussion of the factors affecting debt-servicing costs in OECD countries from 1970 to 1991, see Caselli, Giovannini, and Lane (1998). The

authors conclude that debt-servicing costs depend on a number of variables that affect debt dynamics, such as the primary fiscal balance, the stock of debt outstanding, inflation, and GDP growth. The results were strongest for highly indebted countries.

6. The concept of the importance of the option value of deferring investment decisions is developed in Dixit and Pindyck (1994).

7. Public sector debt as a proportion of GDP will continue to increase if the growth rate of nominal GDP is lower than the growth rate of the debt. The role of the primary deficit or surplus is critical. For example, the ratio of total public sector debt to GDP will increase if the primary deficit is sufficiently large, even though the interest rate on the debt is below the growth rate of GDP.

8. If the debt office is located within the ministry of finance, the formulation of debt management goals and strategy might be undertaken in the middle office within the debt office. The role of the middle office, which is responsible for risk management and portfolio monitoring and control, is discussed more fully in chapter 3.

9. Government debt management operations are usually not large enough to carry out all these functions, but it is common for government debt managers to provide advice in several of these areas.

10. The New Zealand government fully paid down its net foreign currency debt in 1996 as part of its strategy for reducing its overall balance sheet risk. For an indication of how much some European OECD governments reduced their foreign currency exposure in the 1990s, see Favero, Missale, and Piga (2000), which also describes how the share of foreign currency debt in several European government debt portfolios changed after the creation of the European Monetary Union (EMU) and the redenomination of government securities in euros.

11. One exception is Denmark, where the central bank, the Nationalbanken, is authorized to undertake all the government's debt management. Ministry of Finance debt management operations were merged into the Nationalbanken in 1991. In the United Kingdom, foreign currency borrowing by the Bank of England is used to finance the buildup of official reserves.

12. Missale (1999) discusses the policy dimensions of time consistency in relation to public debt management.

13. The welfare costs of high and variable rates of inflation include opportunities forgone because producers are unable to differentiate between general inflation and relative price effects; the redistribution of

wealth to the detriment of those on fixed incomes; and the deadweight losses associated with the variability in tax rates that often follows fiscal and inflationary shocks.

14. Government debt offices in Finland, New Zealand, Sweden, the United Kingdom, the United States, and several other countries require access to forecasts of government spending and revenue flows on a daily basis.

15. The central bank could, for example, review cash flow patterns in previous years to determine whether there is any marked seasonality. Usually, a small number of large government departments account for the main oscillations in liquidity flows (e.g., from tax and customs collection or payment of welfare support).

16. Examples include the debt and budgetary targets set under the Maastricht criteria that supported the moves to establish a European central bank and a common currency. Fiscal policy, public debt targets, or both have been successfully used in recent years to guide macroeconomic policy in Australia, Ireland, New Zealand, the United Kingdom, and the United States. Several countries have established inflation objectives centered on a band of 0–2, 1–3, or 2–4 percent for the annual rate of core or underlying inflation.

Governments sometimes endeavor to meet fiscal targets by bending the rules on classification of fiscal expenditures or by adopting measures that reduce the measured budget deficit but leave government net worth unchanged. See Easterly (1999).

17. In Brazil, the relevant legislation is the Law of Fiscal Responsibility, enacted in 2000. In New Zealand, it is the Fiscal Responsibility Act of 1994.

18. Whereas the objective of many government debt managers is to achieve an acceptable cost and risk structure for the government's debt portfolio, the primary objective of many central banks is price stability, as measured by low and stable rates of underlying inflation.

19. The U.K. Debt Management Office, for example, operates under this type of agreement.

20. For a discussion of direct and indirect instruments of monetary policy and the issues involved in making a transition to more indirect or market-based instruments, see Alexander, Baliño, and Enoch (1995).

21. For extensive coverage of some of the issues involved in coordinating debt management policy and monetary policy in this area, see Sundararajan and others (1994).

Chapter 3

Governance Issues in Managing Government Debt

In the context of government debt management, governance refers to the legal and managerial structure that shapes and directs the operations of government debt managers. It includes the broad legal apparatus (statutory legislation, ministerial decrees, and so on) that defines goals, authorities, and accountabilities. It also embodies the management framework, covering issues such as the formulation and implementation of strategy, operational procedures, quality assurance practices, and reporting responsibilities.

Governance practices differ widely among debt management institutions, whose design reflects the evolution of political settings and public administration practices. Nevertheless, key elements of sound governance for debt management purposes are commonly applicable, and these are described in this chapter.

THE IMPORTANCE OF SOUND GOVERNANCE ARRANGEMENTS

Sound governance practices are essential for government debt management because of the size of government debt portfolios and the balance sheet risks that often accompany them. Government debt portfolios and debt-servicing costs can be very large in relation to GDP (or, for debt-servicing costs, in relation to fiscal aggregates such as annual government tax revenues or spending). Individual borrowing and hedging transactions

49

undertaken by government debt managers, particularly in foreign currency markets, can impose substantial repayment burdens on future generations. Taxpayers therefore want to be certain that these portfolios are being managed soundly, given the fiscal burdens and output adjustments that can accompany substantial portfolio losses or sovereign default. In view of the size of the transactions being managed through various bank accounts, and the scope for misappropriation that exists within systems environments, assurances are needed that an effective system of checks and balances is in place and that the control environment is being regularly reviewed and tested by independent auditors.

Transaction counterparts and investors need to be confident that government debt managers have legal authority to represent the government and that the current government and future governments will stand behind the obligations incurred by the debt managers. Aside from this, investors seek as much certainty and transparency as possible regarding the framework that will guide future government debt management decisions, particularly in relation to cost and risk tradeoffs, borrowing plans, commitments to develop the liquidity of the government bond market, and the regulatory environment (including the tax regime) as it applies to investors.

THE LEGAL FRAMEWORK

Government debt management legislation, along with laws covering the operation of fiscal and monetary policy and the government's auditing functions, is a central element of the governance framework aimed at generating sound financial policies and clear accountabilities. Most governments have in place well-defined legislation relating to the government's powers to borrow, invest, and enter into financial obligations such as guarantees, indemnities, and derivatives transactions and to amortize, redeem, and repurchase government debt. These laws limit potential abuses of power, reduce the possibility of multiple issuers of government debt, and establish appropriate accountabilities for managing the government's debt portfolio.

In most countries the legislation authorizes the minister of finance to conduct all borrowing and related financial transactions on behalf of the government. It also sets the maximum amount of new funding and guarantees that the congress, the parliament, or the minister of finance can approve over a specified period (usually one year).[1] Legislation empowering the minister of finance to manage the government's financial transactions obviates the need to seek specific authorization from the congress or parliament for individual transactions—a requirement that could introduce political considerations into decisionmaking and substantially delay the execution of transactions. A requirement that individual transactions be authorized by the legislature could lead to lengthy delays in negotiating terms and conditions or in deciding which investment bank should be awarded a transaction mandate or from which multilateral development institution the government should borrow.

Empirical studies suggest that budgetary procedures strongly affect fiscal outcomes. Procedures that assign the minister of finance a powerful role in financing decisions and budgetary negotiations invariably lead to better fiscal management than systems that enable the legislature to readily expand the budget and that assign stronger financial powers to ministers with large spending portfolios.[2]

The authority to borrow and manage debt on behalf of the government is often contained within broader public finance legislation outlining the financial management responsibilities of the parliament, ministers, and government agencies. For example, South Africa's Public Finance Management Act of 1999, as amended in the same year, outlines the statutory basis for financial administration in the government and empowers the minister of finance to borrow on behalf of the government. Under this legislation, the minister may borrow to finance national budget deficits, to refinance maturing debt or a loan paid before the redemption date, to obtain foreign currency, to maintain credit balances on a bank account in the National Revenue Fund, to regulate internal monetary conditions should the need arise, or for any other purpose approved by the National Assembly by special resolution (ch. 8, sec. 71).

The debt management component of broader public finance legislation usually outlines the accountabilities of the minister of finance, the debt management institution, or both. It also specifies the roles of the institutions associated with managing the government's debt, such as the parliament, the minister of finance, the ministry of finance, the central bank, and the government audit office. This type of legislation usually contains provisions enabling the minister of finance to delegate to the chief executive of the ministry of finance or to the head of the government's debt management operations the authority to borrow, invest, and enter into other financial commitments on behalf of the government (see box 3).[3]

In deciding how best to implement these authorities, important institution-building considerations arise. If the government is undertaking

---

Box 3
Common elements of legislation on government debt management in developing countries

Although the nature of legislation relating to government debt management differs depending on the political and institutional needs of the country, the U.S. Treasury's Office of Technical Assistance has identified some generally desirable elements. Broadly, such legislation should:

- Affirm that the debt is a direct obligation of the sovereign government as issuer and that it is unconditionally guaranteed by the government
- Establish a limit on total debt issuance
- Create a permanent appropriation for all debt-servicing payments, enabling the government to service debt regardless of the amounts forecast in the annual budget
- Provide a permanent authorization for the payment of issuance and debt service costs and create an authorization to refund all maturing debt
- Grant authority to the minister of finance to act as the sole borrowing agent for the government and enable the minister of finance to select instruments for borrowing and to issue regulations to implement the law
- Provide for equal treatment of investors with respect to all sovereign debt
- Define the relationship between the main organizations involved in government debt management (e.g., the ministry of finance as issuer and the central bank as the fiscal agent)
- Establish an efficient institutional structure to manage the debt (e.g., a debt management office in the ministry of finance or an independent debt management organization) and institute appropriate internal controls within the organization
- Establish the audit and accountability safeguards needed for government debt management.

---

multiple financial transactions, it is inefficient to require that all transactions be approved by the minister of finance. Ministers of finance and their deputy or associate ministers have too many responsibilities to be able to approve every investment and borrowing decision (unless, perhaps, the government seldom borrows in foreign currency). Ministers of finance therefore face choices as to which borrowing and investing powers to delegate, to whom to delegate authority, and how much decisionmaking

---

Box 4
Usual provisions of legislation establishing an autonomous debt management agency

Where debt management agencies have been established under specific legislation, such legislation usually:

- Describes the name, location, and purpose of the agency
- Outlines the functions and responsibilities of the agency
- Empowers the minister of finance to delegate responsibilities to the chief executive of the agency
- Specifies the role and composition of any governing board (e.g., board of advisers) and the procedures relating to compensation and appointments
- Outlines the responsibilities of the chief executive or the head of the organization, including responsibilities regarding personnel issues
- Specifies the reporting requirements in relation to the minister of finance and the parliament
- Indicates the need for transparent and independent auditing arrangements
- Addresses code of conduct–related issues such as obligations with respect to secrecy, disclosure requirements, and avoidance of conflict of interest.

---

authority to vest. These can be difficult decisions, and governments tend to be cautious in making them.

Where governments have established debt management agencies and ministers of finance have delegated many debt management powers to the chief executives of such organizations, governments have sometimes introduced detailed legislation covering the role and accountabilities of the debt agencies.[4] Box 4 outlines some features of such legislation.

Where specific debt management legislation exists, judgment is required as to the degree of specificity of the provisions on individual powers and debt management procedures. Although clarity and transparency are highly desirable, detailed legislation can result in excessive rigidity if it means that all new debt management activities, including the introduction of new financial instruments, have to be covered by new legislation.

Governments need to carefully consider the nature of the legal authorities relating to borrowing decisions to ensure that they do not distort the incentives facing the government's debt managers. For example, in many

**Table 6: Time required to secure approval for borrowing transactions in IBRD borrowing
countries**

	1997 questionnaire		1999 questionnaire	
	Number of countries	Percentage	Number of countries	Percentage
One day or less	0	0	4	10
Less than one week	5	10	5	13
More than one week but less than three months	37	76	26	65
More than three months	7	14	5	13
Total	49	100	40	100

Source: International Bank for Reconstruction and Development (IBRD) Treasury, from questionnaires
completed in preparation for World Bank sovereign debt management forums in October 1997 and
November 1999.

developing countries long-term borrowing decisions are subject to a more
demanding approval system than for short-term borrowing. This can lead to
a bias toward short-term funding and to overreliance on short-term debt. To
illustrate, El Salvador's constitution requires parliamentary approval for any
long-term borrowing, and this has resulted in a disproportionate reliance on
short-term borrowings such as Treasury bills and, consequently, in increased
rollover risk in the government's debt portfolio.

Often, and especially in developing countries, the delays in obtaining
approval for new borrowings can be considerable. In World Bank surveys
of IBRD borrowers, 90 percent of the countries responding in 1997, and
78 percent in 1999, indicated that it took more than a week to obtain government approval to execute a foreign currency borrowing transaction. In
some cases, legislative changes were necessary to effect the borrowing
(table 6).

ESTABLISHING ACCOUNTABILITY FOR GOVERNMENT
DEBT MANAGEMENT

No matter what institutional setting is adopted, the government must be
able to enforce accountability for debt management. Several measures can
help in this regard.

Disclosure of objectives and responsibilities

Public disclosure of the government's debt management objectives and the responsibilities of the government's debt managers is essential for developing a credible debt management mandate and establishing accountability for achieving it. This could be provided through the types of detailed statute that created, for example, Portugal's Instituto de Gestão do Crédito Público and Ireland's National Treasury Management Agency. Alternatively, disclosure could be made through a publicly available document like the U.K. Executive Agency Framework Agreement that outlines the responsibilities of the chancellor and other ministers, the permanent secretary to the Treasury, and the chief executive of the Debt Management Office (DMO). Under this agency agreement, the chancellor of the Exchequer determines the policy and financial framework for the DMO but delegates to the chief executive of the DMO the decisionmaking authority for day-to-day operational matters concerning debt and cash management and for managing the DMO. Where legislation or agency arrangements do not exist, disclosure of the government's debt management objectives can be provided through the publication of annual reports, through presentations or speeches by the minister of finance or senior debt office managers, and by establishing a government debt management website.

Risk management framework

Establishment of a risk management framework and portfolio management policies to guide the decisions of government debt managers is essential for building accountability. Where a government debt agency has been established outside the ministry of finance, recommendations to the minister of finance on the risk management framework should be made by the finance ministry working in conjunction with government debt managers. Often, however, when a debt management office is established outside the ministry of finance, the ministry loses experienced staff to the new agency. The ministry of finance may need to develop specific recruitment and retention strategies to acquire and retain the necessary risk management skills to monitor, oversee, and, when appropriate, partner with the debt office.

Delegation of authority

Where legislation does not outline the responsibilities and authorities of the government debt management unit, a set of financial delegations or approving authorities from the minister of finance to the head of the ministry is required to ensure that the responsibility for implementing debt management is clear.[5] If a debt management agency has been established outside the ministry of finance and the financial powers have not been legislated, the financial delegations would go to the head of the government debt agency. In such circumstances, the head of the finance ministry should advise the minister of finance on the nature of the delegations and should retain authority for advising the government on key debt management policies. All delegations would pass through the head of the debt office to individual portfolio managers and other staff with borrowing or investment responsibilities.

Depending on the complexity and riskiness of the debt portfolio, accountability for performance and compliance can be reinforced by establishing a risk management capability within the debt management operation. Such a unit would monitor and report on performance and on all market, credit, and operational risks and would review whether transactions comply with approved portfolio management policies.

Auditing

Accountability is strengthened by introducing regular auditing of debt management transactions in order to assess their compliance with generally accepted accounting practices and the government's portfolio management policies. A common difficulty in this area is that government auditors may not have sufficient staff with financial market skills to undertake the financial due diligence needed for government debt management (or the financial management of state-owned enterprises). When these services cannot be provided by the government, or if the audit office's fees (if charged) are not competitive, reputable private sector auditors may have to be commissioned to conduct this due diligence.

Reporting

Comprehensive reporting of business-related activities, including financial transactions and audited financial statements, should be provided to the ministry of finance, to the parliament, or to both. The reports should review the government debt managers' business plan, including portfolio performance; assess the risks in the portfolio and compliance with the risk management framework; and discuss how operational risks are being managed.[6]

Oversight by an advisory body

Some governments establish an outside body of advisers (which may be called an advisory committee or board, board of commissioners, or board of directors) to meet regularly and review the operations of the debt management office. Such committees are usually appointed by the government as a means of providing additional quality assurance to the minister of finance (as well as to the head of the ministry of finance or to the head of the debt office) on the management of the debt office. For example, Portugal's Instituto de Gestão do Crédito Público and the Swedish National Debt Office are managed by boards appointed by the government and chaired by the head of the debt office. Advisory boards work with Ireland's National Treasury Management Agency and New Zealand's Debt Management Office.

Advisory boards can be especially valuable when the debt management operation is being created or significantly transformed. In establishing such governance arrangements, it is important to clarify the mandate of the group, its reporting procedures, the membership structure (including the role of the head of the debt office), and compensation arrangements. The mandate and reporting arrangements can be problematic, although there is less difficulty if the group's mandate is mainly to provide oversight and advice across a broad range of operational and related management matters such as the risk management framework, portfolio management policies, systems issues, personnel issues, and audit reports and reviewing budgeting and performance relative to the business plan.

Difficulties concerning the mandate can arise if the group's role extends to reviewing transactions that are underway or proposed. It is common practice to draw some or all members of the advisory board from the private sector (and sometimes from state-owned enterprises) because that is where much of the expertise capable of providing quality assurance on debt management can be found. It is essential, however, to avoid any conflict of interest, whether real or perceived, between the formal role of advisory board members and their private sector interests. Many governments try to avoid the possibility of such conflicts by excluding any review of transaction business and future strategic options from the advisory board's mandate and by selecting members who are unlikely to face any conflict of interest.

For quality assurance to function well, the advisory board should be able to report to the head of the ministry of finance and to have access to the minister of finance when it considers direct communication of its views important. Difficulties can arise if the advisory board is seen by the government debt managers primarily as an alternative adviser on policy issues and business direction, as this can disempower the management and staff within the debt management office and undermine morale. Governments should, nevertheless, have the opportunity to access alternative sources of advice on debt management strategy. It is common practice, especially in OECD countries, to engage outside experts with strong risk management modeling and quantitative skills and comparative country experience to review the government's debt management strategy and risk management framework.[7] These evaluations are often discussed in detail by the advisory board (where there is no conflict of interest) and the debt office and reported to the minister of finance.

Interdepartmental coordination

Governments also seek to raise the quality of debt management and government balance sheet management more generally by establishing interdepartmental committees to share information on financial flows and related policy decisions that affect the management of the government's liquidity. Committees to discuss broad government debt and asset management issues have been established in Belgium, Colombia, Denmark, Hungary, and South Africa. These committees are generally made up of representatives from the government debt management office, the ministry of finance, the central bank, and other agencies such as the prime minister's department or a related body.

HOW MUCH TRANSPARENCY IS DESIRABLE?

Policies are transparent when their objectives are clear and the judgments and the legal and technical facts that support them are made available to the public in an understandable way and on a timely basis. In a debt management context, policy transparency has two major advantages. It reduces market uncertainty as to the objectives of debt management policy, and it creates expectations about the consistency of future policy decisions. This helps build investor confidence and, if matched by greater investor participation, lowers the risk or uncertainty premium embedded in the price of the government's securities. Because decisions by government debt managers can be monitored for consistency with policy goals, transparency also facilitates greater accountability and lower agency costs within the debt office. (Agency costs arise when individuals face incentives to act in a way that differs from the interests of shareholders—in this case, the government. For a discussion of agency costs, see Jensen and Meckling 1976.)

There are no codes or standards specifying the amount of information that debt managers should disclose. At a minimum, governments should disclose the legal architecture surrounding the management of the government's debt, the objectives for debt management, and the debt management strategy. Disclosure of strategic benchmarks is not necessarily required (although several governments do this), but where objectives are expressed in terms of cost, risk, and the development of the domestic government bond market, it should be made clear how cost and risk are being measured and what the specific policy goals are for strengthening the domestic market.

Governments should disclose the size of their borrowing needs for the financial year and any material revisions to this figure. They should also indicate how they intend to finance these needs (e.g., through domestic or foreign currency borrowing) and the tax treatment applicable to any securities. Many governments go further by announcing the auction calendar for the financial year and the expected size of individual auctions. They also indicate which benchmark bonds they will establish and the minimum liquidity they will seek to create in the benchmark securities.

In some situations there will be a tradeoff between disclosure considerations and operational flexibility. This is clearest in cases where full or partial disclosure at an early stage of transactions in the market may turn prices against the debt managers. For example, the debt managers should not disclose their final offer price in buying back a particular foreign currency bond (e.g., through a reverse auction), in case investor demand causes the price of the securities to rise prior to the purchase offer. If the government debt manager is actively trading a liquidity portfolio, it should not reveal which transactions it is contemplating, but it should report the financial returns or losses resulting from such trading. In these situations, the issue is not whether to disclose but when to disclose.

THE INSTITUTIONAL SETTING FOR GOVERNMENT DEBT MANAGEMENT

Many types of institutional arrangements for government debt management are feasible, provided that organizational objectives and roles are clear and there is coordination and sharing of information. In practice, unless there are compelling reasons related to effectiveness, it is not advisable for different agencies to be responsible for the same set of functions.

Concentration of responsibilities

Government debt management generally operates more efficiently if responsibility for decisionmaking and implementation is not spread across several government departments (such as the ministries of finance, planning, and commerce) or across several different departments within the ministry of finance. In many developing countries, however, it is common to find multiple departments with responsibility for managing different parts of the government's debt portfolio (e.g., government cash management, domestic borrowing, guarantees, donor finance, market-related foreign currency borrowing, and borrowing from multilateral development banks). Information requests among different departments in the same ministry can take several months to be answered, and the process can take even longer among ministries.

In most OECD countries, responsibility for government debt management is centralized either within the ministry of finance or in a debt office outside that ministry. When a debt office is established outside the ministry of finance, the ministry should retain the key responsibility for advising the minister of finance on debt management strategy (often in conjunction with the debt office) and for approving important risk management policies or advising the minister on them.[8] In these countries it is also common practice for the central bank to undertake a range of debt management functions for government debt managers.[9] These include conducting daily open market operations in the domestic market as part of liquidity-smoothing operations for cash management purposes, implementing treasury bill and government bond auctions, and maintaining registry services. Where such activities are undertaken on behalf of the government's debt managers, an agency or service agreement is often prepared between the government debt managers and the central bank, as discussed in chapter 2.

In several emerging market countries the central bank manages the government's foreign currency debt portfolio and plays a key role in selling domestic currency debt. Because the central bank manages the foreign currency reserves and interacts extensively with the financial markets in implementing monetary policy, it is often, at least initially, better equipped than the ministry of finance to manage the foreign currency debt portfolio and undertake foreign currency borrowing. Where the central bank exercises these responsibilities, the ministry of finance will need to decide whether to acquire the necessary skills and take over the management of the foreign currency debt portfolio. Irrespective of its implementation role regarding foreign currency debt, the ministry of finance should retain responsibility for advising the government on debt strategy and portfolio and risk management policies relating to both the domestic and foreign currency debt portfolios, given the importance of government debt management for the government's fiscal policy and balance sheet management.

Location of the debt management office

As governments have centralized and upgraded the quality of their debt management, many have established DMOs. These have generally been of two types:

- An office or agency established outside the ministry of finance but reporting to the minister of finance. Such a unit could be established under specific and detailed legislation (examples include the Austrian Federal Financing Agency, Hungary's Debt Management Agency, Ireland's National Treasury Management Agency, and Portugal's Instituto de Gestão do Crédito Público) or as part of broader government machinery involving decrees or policy decisions, as is the case for the Australian Office of Financial Management, Swedish National Debt Agency, and the U.K. Debt Management Office.[10]

- A debt office located within the ministry of finance or the treasury department. Examples include the Treasury of the Kingdom of Belgium, the General Directorate of Public Credit in Colombia, the Department of Finance Canada, Agency France Trésor, and the New Zealand Debt Management Office.[11]

Although responsibility for providing policy advice on debt management strategy should rest with the ministry of finance, there are often marked differences of opinion as to whether the ministry of finance should have operational responsibility for debt management or whether this should be undertaken by a separate debt management office outside the ministry. For developing and emerging market countries that are only beginning to develop the role of government debt management, the arguments for building this competency within the ministry of finance are compelling.

The case for establishing a DMO inside the ministry of finance. Proponents of retaining the implementation role within the ministry of finance cite the nature of the interactions between the ministry's economic and financial forecasting functions and the preparation of the government's borrowing program. At a minimum, debt managers need to understand how the government's financial position is evolving as a result of the government's expenditure and revenue flows, purchases and sales of government assets, and financial transfers to and from state-owned enterprises (SOEs). Debt managers' forecasts of government debt-servicing commitments also feed into the government's budgetary calculations, and information on the government's cash position is required in order to determine the size of, and any amendments to, the government's borrowing program. Although this information could still be exchanged with a debt management office located outside the ministry of finance, it is often more efficient and less risky to develop these interdependencies within the ministry, at least until the government's reputation in debt management is firmly established.

When a new institutional structure for the government's debt management operations is being introduced, senior managers within the ministry of finance need to monitor the work of the office closely. Where management and staff competencies are unproven and a sound risk management culture has yet to emerge, having the debt management office within the ministry of finance makes it easier for the ministry to monitor the work of the office and to take corrective action. For example, senior managers in the finance ministry may wish to shape the development of the risk management culture and to monitor and possibly influence appointments of important managerial personnel such as the head of the debt management office and the managers responsible for portfolio management, risk management, and operations. Although some debt managers might consider this power intrusive, it is desirable that the ministry play a central role in the initial phase in ensuring that, in addition to having the necessary technical skills, senior managers have a good understanding of the public policy considerations involved in debt management and are able to create an operating culture that is consistent with the goals established for the organization.

All of this assumes that the Ministry of Finance is motivated by sound public policy objectives. Difficulties would soon arise, for example, if the Ministry's officials directed that the government debt managers issue large volumes of short maturity debt in the domestic market or borrow extensively in foreign currencies with low interest rates in an attempt to achieve lower debt servicing costs in the short run.

Governments are frequently confronted with capital market issues (often relating to the management of SOEs or their preparation for corporatization or privatization) that require a combination of capital market and public policy advice. From time to time, finance ministers also seek advice on possible financial market reaction to forthcoming economic and financial news (e.g., concerning the budget or revised budget projections). Ministers of finance and heads of the finance ministry often prefer that such advice be readily accessible within the ministry.

The case for establishing a DMO outside the ministry of finance. Advocates of the establishment of a debt agency as a government corporation outside the ministry of finance tend to emphasize two points. The first is the possibility that debt management and cash management might be downplayed within a large institution like a finance ministry, which may give priority to other core activities such as economic forecasting, budget preparation, and analysis of expenditure proposals. Government debt management policy may not receive adequate attention, and the commercial side of the business may not be fully appreciated by senior managers or may not be adequately funded. Staff turnover may be high because of lack of salary competitiveness, internal policies requiring staff to be rotated regularly among jobs within the ministry, or a perception among ministry staff that debt management is not a mainstream activity.

The second argument for establishing a debt office outside the ministry, with oversight by a board of directors or an advisory committee, is that such an institution is likely to be more successful in obtaining budget resources and would adopt more commercial approaches in reviewing the need for additional expenditures on systems, training, salaries, and recruitment. Proponents of this approach also believe that a board or advisory committee would intensively monitor performance and would require considerable transparency in reporting objectives and results. For example, an important benefit of the establishment of the National Treasury Management Agency in Ireland has been the increased focus on and expertise in risk management issues, and this improvement is reflected in the quality of the agency's reporting to the minister of finance.

These benefits can easily be overstated. In practice, the finance ministry is likely to be concerned about the budgetary costs associated with creating and maintaining a debt office outside the ministry, and such an institution may not necessarily receive additional budget resources. The ministry may be uneasy about the signaling effects of allocating a larger budget envelope to such an institution when numerous other government providers of market-related services, such as economic forecasters, tax policy advisers, and health care professionals, face salary competitiveness issues and difficulties in obtaining adequate resources and systems-related funding.

As the government's shareholding representative, the finance ministry may also wish to exercise some control over staff appointments through its representation on any board or advisory committee or by having a right of veto. This can be a difficult area if the governance structure and, in particular, the role of the board are not to be undermined. Where the government has confidence in the government debt managers and has established a debt management office outside the ministry of finance, management and operating decisions, including the appointment of personnel, should normally be entrusted to the board.

Those who advocate the establishment of a debt management office outside the ministry of finance also emphasize the importance of separating responsibility for fiscal policy advice (with its influence on interest rates) from responsibility for debt management. They believe, correctly, that any perception of market manipulation or insider trading would be damaging to the government, the ministry of finance, the debt management office, and the domestic financial market.

This point would be an important concern if government debt managers were issuing domestic currency debt opportunistically and trading it in the local market. Although firewalls could be erected so that the debt managers had no inside information on changes in fiscal or monetary policy, the market may have doubts as to the effectiveness of the separation. Even if government debt managers are not trading domestic currency debt, they still need to be sensitive to the fact that bondholders have invested in securities issued by them as agents of the government. Bondholders would be very concerned if they felt that government debt managers were using inside information to manipulate the pricing of bonds. But in practice, few governments permit their debt managers to trade government debt actively in the domestic market, as distinct from arranging buybacks of off-the-run issues for liquidity management purposes, and many governments have successfully conducted government debt management operations from within the ministry of finance without raising concerns about conflicts of interest or insider trading.

CONTRIBUTION OF THE DMO TO A BROADER PERSPECTIVE ON MANAGEMENT OF A GOVERNMENT BALANCE SHEET

Debt management offices that are housed within the ministry of finance have sometimes been merged into a broader organizational structure charged with providing advice on the management of risk across the government's balance sheet. For example, the New Zealand Debt Management Office, which reports to the minister of finance through the chief executive of the New Zealand Treasury, forms part of the Treasury's Asset and Liability Management Branch. The asset side of the branch provides advice on the privatization of government assets (including the management of the sale process) and on the restructuring of SOEs. It also advises on the management of a wide range of commercial, contractual, and litigation risks on behalf of the government. South Africa's National Treasury has established a similar office, as described in box 5.

Box 5
Development of the Asset and Liability Management Branch, South Africa

Before the establishment in 1996 of the Asset and Liability Management Branch in South Africa's National Treasury (then called the Department of Finance), responsibility for managing the central government's debt and its financial assets was fragmented. Foreign currency borrowing was undertaken by the South African Reserve Bank, with the Department of Finance having little input into the decisions. Foreign currency loans, however, were managed within the Department of Finance, and responsibility for different aspects of the government's cash management was spread across several government agencies. The government's accessing of financial markets was uncoordinated; little oversight of state-owned enterprises (SOEs) was conducted; requests for government guarantees for borrowings by SOEs were on the rise; and understanding of the full nature of the government's asset and liability portfolios was limited.

A key reform in reorganizing the Department of Finance was to establish the Asset and Liability Management Branch and to begin phasing in responsibility for policy advice, monitoring, and reporting on the government's assets and liabilities. The branch's asset management responsibilities currently include providing advice regarding corporate governance, management of risk exposures relating to SOEs, and the restructuring and privatization of SOEs. On the debt management side, the branch is responsible for the government's cash management and for managing the central government's domestic and foreign currency debt.

The South African Reserve Bank provides debt management services to the Asset and Liability Management Branch, including execution of bill and bond auctions and participation in the supervision of primary dealers,

(Box continues on the following page.)

> **Box 5** (continued)
>
> and the bank also manages the government's foreign currency reserves. A committee made up of officials from the Department of Finance and the South African Reserve Bank exchanges information and discusses ways to improve coordination. An additional public debt management committee consisting of advisers from the Budget Office, the Office of the Accountant General, the South African Reserve Bank, and the Asset and Liability Management Branch meets regularly to discuss budgetary, debt management, and cash management issues.
>
> The creation of the Asset and Liability Management Branch has led to major gains, including the introduction of an integrated government balance sheet, much greater shareholder oversight of the risks associated with the government's asset and liability portfolios, establishment of sound corporate governance protocols, and more coordinated accessing of financial markets. It has also produced better and more uniform government policies regarding SOEs, which has helped promote stronger financial performance and sounder risk management practices by these enterprises, and it has brought about improved policy coordination among monetary policy, budgetary policy, and debt management policy.
>
> *Source:* Coen Kruger, deputy director general, Asset and Liability Management Branch, Department of Finance: Address to the Second IBRD Sovereign Debt Management Forum, Washington, D.C., November 1–3, 1999.

Two major benefits arise from this type of organizational structure. First, by improving the understanding of risks on the government's balance sheet, it encourages ministers, as well as policy advisers within the ministry of finance and in the government at large, to consider the full balance sheet implications of policy proposals rather than their effect on the government's asset or liability portfolio in isolation. Policymakers can more readily assess their ownership interests within such a balance sheet framework. They become more conscious of the balance sheet effects of investing in and divesting government assets and of whether policy decisions can be expected to increase or reduce the government's net worth or increase its overall risk.

Second, the structure allows the identification of natural hedges in the government's balance sheet that may lead to savings in transaction costs.[12]

For example, different government agencies may be handling financial issues that have both asset and liability management aspects or government entities may be attempting to hedge risks through the private sector when an offsetting natural hedge exists elsewhere in the government's balance sheet. Or, large cumulative exposures, possibly of a contingent nature, may come to light that previously were incorrectly reported and that are unacceptable to the government.

One of the key organizational issues is to decide how broad the responsibilities of government debt managers should be in managing parts of the government's balance sheet. At a minimum, government debt managers need to have policy responsibility for managing the domestic and foreign currency debt of the central government, even if some of the implementation is contracted out to the central bank. But difficult issues can arise in deciding whether to extend the government debt managers' mandate to funding and managing risks associated with the government's investment in SOEs, particularly those with commercial objectives, and whether debt managers' role should include monitoring and managing risk relating to the government's contingent liabilities. The latter issue is discussed in chapter 6.

Several alternatives are possible for managing the funding and risk management functions of SOEs. One option, adopted by many emerging market countries, is to have government debt managers undertake all borrowing on behalf of the government and on-lend the funds to SOEs, which manage the market risk. This takes advantage of the government's credit rating (which is often superior to that of the SOEs) and its stronger name recognition among investors. Central management of the borrowing program helps build up "benchmark" bond issues and improve the liquidity of the government bond market.

Central management is likely to result in lower borrowing costs, but it can run counter to a desire for an arm's-length relationship between the government and SOEs.

An alternative approach is to permit SOEs to borrow in their own name, subject to borrowing conditions or risk management constraints imposed by the government, as has been done in Colombia. Having established foreign currency, interest rate, and liquidity benchmarks for its own debt portfolio, the Colombian government sets the same liability benchmarks for the foreign currency exposures of its SOEs, with the aim of ensuring that the desired liability structure for a substantial part of the government's balance sheet is not being undermined by the SOEs' treasury activities.

Many other governments permit SOEs to borrow in the capital markets without restriction. These SOEs will experience higher borrowing costs if their credit rating is below the government's or if issuance activities have limited liquidity. The practice does, however, have the benefit of creating more of an arm's-length relationship between the government and the SOEs and, as discussed below, avoids the need for any precommitment by the government as to future shareholder support. It also introduces private sector monitoring of the performance of the SOEs, which can help reduce risk and improve shareholder return.

Alternatively, some combination of these approaches might be used. For example, the SOE may be permitted to borrow in the domestic market, but the government's debt managers might undertake all of the foreign currency borrowing and manage the associated risks. Or, if the government is trying to reduce its overall foreign currency exposure, it may require the SOE to borrow solely in domestic currency (unless the enterprise generates sufficient foreign currency revenues to service foreign currency borrowing).

Which approach is preferable will depend on a balance of considerations relating to the potential cost savings from central funding, the importance of the government's governance objectives for SOEs, and whether any signal by the government of future shareholder support would undermine these governance objectives. A range of approaches is found internationally.

A governance framework aimed at creating or promoting conditions for a successful business enterprise—meaning, for example, that the enterprise operates without competitive advantages or disadvantages and that managers are free to make all management decisions even though they remain accountable to ministers or to a government-appointed board of directors— would probably result in the SOE's managing its own borrowing program.[13] In view of its 100 percent ownership interest in the SOE, the government would need to carefully review the entity's business and financing plan and be prepared to veto decisions if it believed that the business strategy and proposals for asset and liability management were inappropriate.[14]

If the SOE wishes to borrow in the international capital markets, the sovereign credit rating agencies will seek to ascertain the shareholder's (i.e., the government's) intentions with respect to future financial support should the enterprise subsequently face insolvency. This can present a dilemma for the government. It may wish to avoid the moral hazard problem of indicating to SOE managers that it would provide financial support for the enterprise in the event of poor managerial performance.[15] Yet an unwillingness to provide such an assurance to the sovereign credit rating agencies would result in the SOE's being rated on its balance sheet strength alone. This could mean a lower credit rating and higher funding costs.

If the government's objective is to ensure that the SOE operates in a competitive environment and that SOE managers face incentives and accountabilities that encourage strong managerial performance, it should avoid providing assurances of future capital injections in the event of business failure. If, however, the government's policy is to underwrite the performance of SOEs, it may prefer that borrowing be centralized (especially if the government has a higher credit rating than the subborrower or the SOE) to take advantage of government debt managers' portfolio management skills and market knowledge.

THE ORGANIZATION OF THE DMO

Sound governance considerations suggest that debt management functions should be consolidated in one location and organised along functional lines. Accordingly, nearly all debt management offices have adopted an organizational structure similar to that found in leading corporate and banking treasuries and in the reserve asset management departments of many central banks. Functional responsibilities for managing transactions are divided among offices within the debt management organization, and procedures are established to ensure internal control and accountability. Usually, this involves the creation of front, middle, and back offices and of separate reporting lines to the head of the debt office. (Sometimes these offices are referred to as the portfolio management team, risk management team, and treasury operations team.)

The front office

The front office (the portfolio management team) is normally responsible for the analysis and efficient execution of all portfolio transactions, consistent with the portfolio management policy of the debt office. Front-office activities include producing cash flow projections (often in partnership with the middle office), borrowing in domestic and foreign currencies, designing and executing trading and hedging transactions, and investing foreign currency liquidity and any excess cash balances associated with the government's daily departmental cash management. Within the front office, individual portfolio managers are usually assigned different functional responsibilities (e.g., medium-term foreign currency borrowing in certain currencies, liquidity management, or domestic currency funding) on an instrument, market, or currency basis. Portfolio managers are responsible for managing their banking relationships, although questions of how much credit exposure to assign different counterparties are decided in the middle office.

Because front-office portfolio managers work closely with the market, they are able to offer a wide range of portfolio management services, including design of funding, hedging, investment, and buyback strategies; assessment of fair value on individual transactions; and exploration of market opportunities to help move the actual debt portfolio closer to the strategic benchmarks.[16] They can also provide advice on matters such as the proposed balance sheet restructuring of SOEs, government policy initiatives to foster the development of the primary and secondary government bond markets, and possible market reaction to new fiscal information.

The middle office

A middle office, or risk management team, is normally responsible for establishing a cost and risk management strategy or framework for the government's debt portfolio, researching and analyzing policy alternatives, and monitoring compliance with the portfolio and risk management policies. In some countries these responsibilities cover broad obligations on the government's balance sheet, including guarantees and other contingent liabilities and the monitoring of private sector foreign currency debt (which can represent a possible contingent liability). Risk management policies are discussed in chapter 5.

The head of the middle office often advises the head of the debt management office on objectives for government debt management and on the cost and risk tradeoffs of various portfolio management strategies. The risk analysis needed to develop and review the strategy frequently draws on the analytical techniques referred to in chapter 5. Starting from the government's preferences with respect to expected cost and risk, middle-office staff develop a set of portfolio management policies, discuss these with the ministry of finance (if the debt office is not within the ministry), and seek the approval of the minister of finance. Usually, the portfolio management policy documentation specifies the government's debt management objectives, describes the portfolio-related and operational risks that need to be managed, and outlines in detail the policies and procedures for addressing these risks.

On the compliance side, the middle office typically produces regular reports monitoring market and credit risk and comparing overall risk exposures with the acceptable tolerances specified in the portfolio management policy. Portfolio returns from any active trading are reviewed and assessed on a risk-adjusted basis.

Middle offices essentially perform a mixture of research, analysis, due diligence and reporting functions. Some, like the Belgian, Irish, and Swedish debt offices, also contain a legal unit. Information technology functions can be a middle-office responsibility but tend to be located in the back office. Some middle offices (in Belgium, Brazil, and Colombia, for example) also have investor relations functions, but usually this is a front-office responsibility.

Middle offices are particularly valuable when there is a substantial foreign currency debt or foreign currency liquidity portfolio and when the government's debt management includes transactions such as managing against a strategic benchmark, tactical trading, hedging strategies, and buyback operations. Even when the debt portfolio is entirely in domestic currency, however, a middle office could analyze issues such as the desired interest rate sensitivity of the domestic currency portfolio, the expected cost and risk from introducing new debt instruments, the desirable number and liquidity of benchmark bonds, and the best method of selling domestic currency bonds.

Extensive interaction between the front and middle offices is necessary, but the respective responsibilities of the two groups can lead to tensions. The middle office's responsibilities for recommending an appropriate risk management and control environment and for undertaking due diligence and performance reporting can run counter to the transaction-oriented culture of the front office. These tensions can arise, for example, in considering whether to undertake new types of transactions or introduce new instruments, in setting portfolio benchmarks, and in measuring and reporting value added.

It is important to address these tensions and to maintain a balance that preserves the integrity of both functions. For example, an oppressive system of monitoring and compliance can stifle the initiative of front-office staff in their search for ways to add value to the debt management operation through lower debt-servicing costs, increased returns from liquidity management, or reduced risk. Similarly, the integrity of the middle-office staff and their pride in their responsibilities for risk management design and for monitoring and control can be seriously compromised if this group is not given sufficient freedom to develop its professional capacity. An essential step in resolving these tensions is to ensure that there is agreement on and respect for the essential roles of the two offices and their capacity to develop strong synergies within a clear set of accountabilities.

The back office

Back-office (treasury operations) responsibilities usually include confirming trades, issuing payment instructions for transactions, accounting for trades, arranging collateral transfers, administering loan documentation, and managing relationships with fiscal agents (which, for domestic debt, may be the central bank) and with registrars and paying agents. Responsibility for managing the systems needs of the debt office, including systems planning, implementation of new systems, and maintenance and updating of existing applications, is also usually assigned to this office. Compilation of debt statistics and reporting on operational risk or vulnerabilities—often, with the help of the middle office—is frequently a back-office responsibility.

Considerable checks and balances should be introduced in the operation of the back office. Some of the largest financial losses in banks have occurred when the management of these responsibilities and accountabilities has broken down.[17] In order to maintain tight internal controls, there must be clear procedures regarding the entry of transactions into the loan accounting or management information systems, the checking of these transactions, and the confirmation and issuing of payment instructions. For example, portfolio managers should not enter trades into the management information system (unless the system can recognize a status of less than fully confirmed, in which case trades would enter the debt database once settlement staff had processed external confirmations). Nor should they issue payment instructions to the settlement banks. Staff booking the transactions should not be able to approve payment, and those authorizing payment should not be responsible for financial reporting. For these reasons, back-office staff have carefully delineated performance and backup functions and documented procedures.

Treasury operations require highly professional staff. Within financial intermediaries, however, there is often a tendency to undervalue their role. Unless measures are adopted to address this attitude, serious divisions can develop in the organizational culture, undermining the morale of the back-office team and leading to high staff turnover.

REINFORCING THE ORGANIZATIONAL STRUCTURE THROUGH SOUND APPOINTMENTS AND A STRONG CODE OF ETHICS

Within a government debt management office, the most important appointed personnel are the head of the debt management office and the managers in charge of the front, middle, and back offices. Among them, they manage important relationships that involve the minister of finance; banks, investors and other financial market participants; the sovereign credit rating agencies; the advisory board (if one exists) of the office or agency; the central bank; and the media. They are responsible for ensuring that the government debt office's behavior and style of transacting are exemplary. Given that market participants will closely monitor and analyze the office's transactions and decisions, each of these appointees has substantial responsibilities that can pose a reputational risk for government debt management operations and, in some instances, for the minister of finance and the domestic financial market.

In allocating transaction mandates, and especially borrowing mandates, government debt managers make decisions that are of high value to investment banks. Given the size of transaction fees and the pressures on banks to be seen as leaders in market segments, as reflected in various league tables, financial intermediaries such as investment banks compete aggressively for transaction mandates from governments, especially borrowing and hedging-related mandates. Negotiations with banks may involve substantial international travel, hospitality, and gifts. Decisions as to whether to borrow in foreign or domestic currency or to whom to award borrowing mandates should not be swayed by hospitality or special interests but should be based on objective criteria such as pricing (including fees), execution capacity, distribution coverage, and the value that the intermediary brings to the relationship in the form of other transactions, information, advice, and new ideas.

Establishing an in-house code of ethics that provides guidance on conduct with respect to matters such as the management of personal financial portfolios, relationships with counterparties, and the acceptance of gifts and hospitality can be valuable for establishing suitable standards of behavior. But the development of a strong risk management culture within a debt office comes more from a thorough understanding of the commercial standards and requirements of government debt management and the important and often subtle interface with public policy goals in a range of transactional, relationship management, and reporting functions. The head of the debt office and the managers responsible for portfolio management, risk management, and operations can exert a major influence in enforcing ethical standards and in fostering a strong risk management culture within the office. This is one of their most important responsibilities.

Senior government debt managers need to have not only the sound judgment and well-developed skills that are important for other public sector managers but also an excellent knowledge of the technical aspects of the businesses for which they are responsible. This is especially so in view of the financial skills and background of the market counterparties with whom they deal, managers' responsibility for training and developing staff within the debt office, and the potential for fraudulent market transactions such as prime bank notes and for fraud within the debt office. Finally, managers' skills and knowledge need to be commensurate with the magnitude of their overall responsibility for what is usually the largest financial portfolio in the country and a central component of the government's balance sheet.

NOTES

1. Sometimes, multiyear targets are established in the form of a preset limit or debt ceiling.

2. These results were strongly supported in Latin American and OECD economies; see Alesina and others (1999).

3. If the minister of finance is the chief executive of the ministry of finance or the treasury department, the delegation might go directly to the position directly responsible for heading the debt management operations. Normally, when the minister is not also the chief executive, accountability will be delegated to the head or chief executive of the ministry and be subdelegated, in full or in part, to the manager with overall responsibility for these functions.

4. In Ireland and Portugal, the legislation relates specifically to the establishment of the National Treasury Management Agency and the Instituto de Gestão do Crédito Público, respectively.

5. If the minister is also the head of the ministry, the delegation might go directly to the manager responsible for managing the government's debt.

6. Excellent annual reports, for example, are prepared by the government debt management institutions in Brazil, Colombia, Denmark, Ireland, Portugal, Sweden, and the United Kingdom.

7. For example, extensive reviews of debt management strategy using outside consultants have been undertaken in Colombia (1995), Belgium (1996), New Zealand (1996), Ireland (1998), Sweden (1998), and Australia (1999).

8. In general, the approval of the minister of finance should be sought for the overall portfolio management policy framework, including risk management policies. The minister's approval should be obtained for major modifications to these policies, but minor policy changes could be ratified by the ministry of finance.

9. In other countries, such as France, Sweden, and the United Kingdom, these functions are carried out by the debt office.

10. The U.K. Debt Management Office was established as an executive agency of the Treasury on April 1, 1998. The responsibilities of Treasury ministers, the permanent secretary to the Treasury, and the chief executive of the DMO are specified in a published framework document that also identifies strategic objectives and accountabilities with respect to reporting to Parliament.

11. The Australian Office of Financial Management, for example, was established as a prescribed agency under general legislation conferring financial and resource management responsibilities and governance responsibilities on the chief executive of the agency. The decree founding Agency France Trésor was signed by the minister of economy, finance, and industry in February 2001.

12. For example, in New Zealand five separate units within the government were responsible for managing the financial flows arising from membership in the IMF. No single unit had overall responsibility for risk management. This became apparent when hedging activities by one institution, based on its own balance sheet exposure, turned out to be suboptimal from the perspective of the government's overall balance sheet. Another New Zealand example involves the Earthquake Commission (EQC), a government-owned entity that collects premiums from households for an earthquake insurance fund. The EQC, which had government approval to invest in foreign currency government bonds (held by the central bank as part of its foreign currency reserves) on a hold-to-maturity basis, wished to purchase currency options from the private sector to safeguard itself against an appreciation in the New Zealand dollar and a decline in the marked-to-market value of the bonds. The hold-to-maturity aspect of the investment made this hedging inappropriate, and since the government had zero net foreign currency debt (that is, its foreign currency

debt and foreign currency reserves were fully currency and interest rate matched), any change in the marked-to-market value of the EQC's foreign exchange assets was fully offset by a change in the marked-to-market value of the government's foreign currency debt. Hedging part of the government's balance sheet with the private sector, when natural hedges existed, would have been costly and unnecessary. (These examples were provided to the Second IBRD Sovereign Debt Management Forum, Washington, D.C., November 1–3, 1999, by Phillip Anderson, treasurer of the New Zealand Debt Management Office.)

13. These measures could include establishing a debt-to-equity ratio similar to those maintained by private sector firms operating in the same industry or reducing restrictions on procurement and hiring policies.

14. In this type of model, SOE managers would be empowered to develop business plans that are consistent with the government's ownership objectives and to manage the enterprise's physical, human, and intellectual capital accordingly.

15. In this instance, *moral hazard* refers to the incentive for increased risk taking that can arise when institutions are protected from the risk of bankruptcy because of likely government support. More generally, moral hazard exists when the interests of the owner of a resource are not well aligned with those of the individual managing it, creating incentives for excessive risk taking or other forms of opportunistic behavior.

16. For example, by negotiating terms for new borrowings and developing hedging strategies and buyback opportunities.

17. One of the most serious examples was the Barings affair, in which financial losses by the Singapore branch of Barings Bank led to the collapse and takeover of the institution. A Singapore-based Barings trader had ready access to back-office applications at Barings Singapore. Without authority, the trader maintained overnight positions, exceeded intraday trading limits, and took very large exposures in equity-based options (which were only permitted if the trader was transacting as an execution broker on behalf of clients). In the London headquarters the back-office functions were not effectively monitored, and the reporting lines to the trader were not clear. Gross trading limits for these trading activities had not been established, and there was inadequate understanding in London as to whether requests for cash by the Singapore office were for client positions or for house trading. These findings are discussed in Bank of England (1995).

Chapter 4

Managing Government Debt in an Asset-and-Liability Management Framework

As discussed in chapter 1, most OECD governments express their debt management objectives in terms of expected cost and risk. These objectives become operationalized through the portfolio and risk management policies within the debt office. But what do cost and risk mean for a government debt portfolio, and how can governments determine their risk preferences and assess the tradeoff between expected cost and risk?

Risk and uncertainty are closely related concepts. Uncertainty arises when multiple outcomes are possible, and risk is concerned with the consequences of uncertainty. Risk refers to the expected negative effects or pain that could arise from an unfavorable or undesirable outcome. It has two main elements: the likelihood or probability that a negative outcome might occur, and the magnitude of the negative effects associated with the possible range of outcomes.

It may not be possible to estimate risk accurately. For example, in selecting a business partner or a spouse, risk assessment could be used to review possible outcomes under different scenarios, but emotional attachment and judgment about personal qualities and values are likely to be crucial to the decisionmaking process.

The uncertainties associated with risk are highly relevant to investment decisionmaking. Sometimes, though, risk itself is confused with the risk assessment process. Because the cash flows associated with financial securities (or portfolios of securities) can be projected under different assumptions, using an array of statistical measures of volatility derived from historical cash flows, it is often supposed that risk analysis reduces overall risk. This kind of thinking is based on an assumption that the future will be similar to the past, and it can lead to overconfidence among investors when deciding on asset classes, selecting investment instruments, and determining holding periods. Scenario building and statistical analysis are essential elements of the risk assessment process and are valuable tools for constructing a policy framework for managing risk, but they do not eliminate risk, which remains a central element in decisionmaking.

GOVERNMENT TOLERANCE FOR RISK

Governments tend to be risk averse; they have a low appetite or tolerance for risk. Accordingly, they generally seek to avoid making policy decisions, including financial ones, where unfavorable outcomes can have serious negative consequences. Governments' preference for less risk is often revealed by their decisions to downsize their balance sheets, privatize state-owned entities, reduce their contingent liabilities and by their conservatism in analyzing private sector proposals for sharing risk.

There are several reasons for government aversion to risk. Taxpayers or "representative voters" tend to be risk averse in their own decisionmaking and expect the government to have a similar risk preference in managing its financial interests. (See, for example, Palsson 1996.) Governments are less likely to be criticized for forgoing opportunities because of a risk-averse approach than for losing money as a result of risky strategies.

Governments are also concerned about the effects that large portfolio losses could have on their fiscal positions, their borrowing costs, and, potentially, their access to capital. Such losses increase debt-servicing costs and eventually lead to higher tax rates or to spending cuts. Although the quality of public debt management may not, by itself, cause a government to default, it can exacerbate a crisis and constrain the choice and effectiveness of corrective policies. High and rising tax rates have political costs, and they reduce individuals' incentives and willingness to work, save, and invest.

Furthermore, individuals have limited ability, especially in the short run, to foresee and undo the financial consequences arising from poor financial decisions by the government. They frequently lack detailed information about the government's portfolio management decisions, and they may not have access to appropriate hedging instruments or know how to apply them. As demonstrated by the financial crises in East Asia and Russia in the late 1990s, the adjustment burdens resulting from poor financial management fall disproportionately on citizens with the least ability to bear them.

Not all countries share this risk preference. Risk tolerance can change depending on the government's philosophy and the economic circumstances. Some literature on fiscal policy suggests that the quality of decision-making in respect of government expenditure can deteriorate as public finances improve, especially when fiscal surpluses have been achieved. This can extend to a greater willingness to take risk. A greater appetite for risk could be manifested in, say, speculative investments in energy exploration or joint ventures in high-risk activities with private sector partners. On the debt management front, it could involve tactically trading a liquidity portfolio or basing all borrowing decisions on views about future movements in exchange rates and interest rates. A government also might become less risk averse and increasingly seek to finance speculative spending through expensive borrowing, if it believes it is facing the prospect of default.

COST OF DEBT

In a government debt management context, financial cost refers to the effect that servicing debt obligations over the medium and long run has on the government's budget. This is usually measured by the future stream of nominal debt-servicing costs, which include payments of interest and principal. If the government has difficulty in rolling over its debt or is forced to default, the associated economic losses should be counted as part of the cost of managing the debt portfolio. If the government trades part of its debt portfolio in an attempt to produce additional risk-adjusted returns, the financial results from trading should be assessed by measuring the change in the marked-to-market value of the portfolio over the trading period.

INSIGHTS FROM THE ECONOMIC LITERATURE ON THE OPTIMAL STRUCTURE OF GOVERNMENT DEBT

The economic literature on optimal taxation explores the question of whether a government debt portfolio should be structured so as to hedge the government's budgetary position from economic shocks. This literature concludes that governments should seek to smooth tax rates over time because of the effects of distortions created by high and variable tax rates. These distortions ("deadweight losses") arise because individuals' decisions on how long to work, what amount to save, and how best to invest are less optimal than they would be in the absence of changes in tax rates. Since the mid-1980s, much of the tax reform undertaken by national administrations has been driven by concern about high and inequitable tax rates and their effect on individuals' desire to work and save.

Economies regularly experience economic shocks, and the more serious shocks can significantly alter an economy's growth path and a government's budgetary position. Governments borrow to smooth out the impact of these disturbances and avoid making large changes in tax rates or in government spending. The literature discusses whether the structure or composition of a government debt portfolio can be used to hedge the government's budgetary position from economic shocks. It also explores whether the currency composition and interest rate basis of new government borrowing affect inflationary expectations in the private sector and therefore the rate of output growth achievable for a given growth rate of nominal income.

An effective budgetary hedge would cause government debt-servicing costs to co-vary with government tax revenue during the economic shock. The literature suggests that a government debt portfolio consisting of nominal fixed-rate debt can help protect the government's budgetary position in case of supply-side shocks. For example, an economy heavily dependent on oil imports and experiencing a substantial rise in oil prices would see its price level rise, its output decline, and budget revenues decrease. The deterioration in the fiscal accounts would be moderated if the government's debt-servicing costs were fixed in nominal terms and declined in real terms. If, instead, the government debt portfolio consisted of inflation-indexed debt or variable-rate debt, the budgetary position would deteriorate as tax revenue fell and debt-servicing costs increased. Similarly, if the exchange rate depreciated in response to the rise in oil prices, the fiscal situation would worsen if the government debt portfolio contained foreign currency debt or foreign currency–indexed debt.

Other supply-side shocks, such as an unfavorable shock to productivity (stemming, for example, from internal strife or war) would also increase prices and reduce aggregate output. A portfolio of fixed-rate debt would help hedge the budgetary impact.

Inflation-indexed debt and variable-interest-rate debt are better hedges than fixed-rate debt in the case of demand shocks. If, for example, households were to significantly reduce their demand for money or increase their savings rate, it could be expected that inflation, output growth, and tax revenues would decline in the short and medium term. The government's debt-servicing costs would be lower if the government debt portfolio contained inflation-indexed or variable-rate debt; they would remain unchanged in nominal terms (and be higher in real terms) if the debt portfolio consisted of fixed-rate debt.

It is sometimes argued that issuing fixed-rate domestic bonds creates incentives for time-inconsistent government behavior—that is, the government could be led to depart from its stated policies and to accept higher rates of inflation or impose higher tax rates on investors in order to reduce the real level of its debt-servicing commitments. Investors recognize this possibility and consequently require higher yields in order to invest in government instruments. Governments can avoid or lower this risk premium by issuing inflation-indexed debt, variable-rate debt, short-term debt, or foreign currency-indexed debt. Investors believe that these debt instruments give governments less incentive to act opportunistically as higher-than-anticipated inflation would be quickly reflected in higher debt-servicing costs.

The choice of debt instrument that a government should issue largely depends on the structure of the economy, the type of economic shocks most frequently experienced, and the nature of the institutional demand for government securities. In practice, OECD governments issue relatively few types of debt instrument, confining themselves mainly to domestic currency fixed-rate bonds and treasury bills. Inflation-indexed securities, where they are used, usually account for less than 15 percent of government debt. The reasons for the relatively small proportion of inflation-indexed securities are discussed in chapter 9. Unless they are rolling over maturing foreign currency debt or financing foreign currency reserves, OECD governments avoid issuing foreign currency debt or having a high proportion of short-maturity debt in their debt portfolios.

Valuable insights for identifying a preferred debt structure can be obtained by looking at government debt management within a broader asset and liability management framework. The next two sections explore how the private sector uses such a framework and examine the application to government debt management.

ASSET AND LIABILITY MANAGEMENT FRAMEWORK FOR FINANCIAL INTERMEDIARIES

Financial intermediaries' balance sheets usually contain diverse financial assets such as fixed-income products, equities, real estate, and loan receivables that have been financed by deposits, borrowings, and equity. These assets and financial claims have cash flow streams whose value will change as a result of interest rate and exchange rate movements.

Market risk in the balance sheets of financial intermediaries can be measured by the extent to which mismatches in the cash flows of the assets and liabilities exist. The balance sheet will be immunized when the sensitivity of the asset and liability cash flows to changes in interest rates is equal. When the financial policy of the institution is to maintain this immunization over time, continuous hedging transactions ("dynamic hedging") may be needed to offset the effects of changes in interest rates and exchange rates on the value of cash flows.

A financial intermediary would be taking substantial risk, for example, if it borrowed long-term, fixed-rate funding and lent on a floating-rate basis—that is, if it priced its loans off a floating interest rate benchmark such as the London interbank offered rate (LIBOR), adding a fixed spread to cover operating overhead, provisions for bad debts, and a profit margin. In this situation, the intermediary could substantially reduce its risk by using the swap market to convert its fixed-rate borrowings into floating-rate debt and by ensuring that the currency composition of its borrowings (after swaps) matched the currency in which it lent.

The intermediary would still be exposed to risk if the final maturity of its borrowings and loans differed. If the maturity of its loans exceeded that of its borrowings, the intermediary would face refinancing risk—the risk that the cost of the new borrowing (on an after-swap, floating-rate basis) required to refinance maturing debt would be more expensive than the earlier floating-rate debt and that the price of existing loans could not be adjusted to offset the higher cost.[1] Such a situation could occur if the intermediary had maturity mismatches in its borrowing and lending portfolios and its credit rating declined, raising the cost of borrowing and swapping into floating-rate debt. To protect against this risk, it would be prudent for the intermediary to incorporate a risk premium in the lending spread on its loans and to use the additional income to build up its financial reserves. Alternatively, the institution could build a provision into its loan contracts enabling it to adjust the lending spread at regular intervals.

By using such analysis, financial intermediaries can determine the degree of balance sheet risk most appropriate for their business and can actively manage this risk through their treasury operations.

ASSET AND LIABILITY MANAGEMENT FRAMEWORK FOR A GOVERNMENT

In many respects, government financial management responsibilities are comparable to those of a large diversified private sector corporation. Governments, for example, receive revenue (including interest and dividends), make cash payments, borrow in institutional and retail markets, manage diversified financial portfolios of assets and liabilities, service debt, make new loans and guarantees, invest in and divest real estate, and establish and liquidate entities.

There are, of course, important differences between the two types of institution. Large diversified private sector companies have different risk and return objectives and a complex capital structure. Managers have strong incentives to achieve financial objectives, given the markets' focus on quarterly financial performance and the fact that the institution's equity can readily be bought and sold. Governments have broader responsibilities: they provide public goods and services (defense, education, health care, and so on) that benefit all citizens, or large numbers of them, and they fulfill important regulatory and economic management roles.

Governments, like individuals, could conceptually produce balance sheets that reflect their assets, claims against the assets, and net worth. In fact, few governments periodically prepare a balance sheet, but they nevertheless own assets and incur liabilities and could do so.[2]

A government's main financial asset is usually the flow of tax revenue it expects to receive over several years. (In some countries it might be the stream of commodity revenues it anticipates receiving until the asset is depleted.) Other important government assets include loan receivables (as a result of on-lending to state governments, to publicly and privately owned companies, and to individuals); foreign exchange reserves; cash holdings at the central bank; and infrastructural investments in, for example, transport networks, energy production and distribution, education and health, and security-related assets.

The main claims against a government are the cash outlays it expects to make over time in providing goods and services (including income transfers) and its outstanding loans and guarantees. Governments also have equity interests in state-owned enterprises such as publicly owned companies and corporations; equity in international financial institutions, including the IMF, the World Bank, and regional development institutions (which also give rise to sizeable contingent liabilities); and joint-venture arrangements with private investors.[3] Figure 1 illustrates a typical set of government assets and liabilities.

Governments incur financial and credit risks in carrying out their broad economic, regulatory, and public good functions. Examination of the nature of the assets and obligations that the government manages, and of the types of financial flows associated with them, can be a valuable guide for managing government balance sheet risk. In practice, this involves considering the nature of the cash flows generated by the government's assets and assessing their sensitivity to factors such as changes in real interest rates, currency movements, and shifts in the terms of trade; it does not require valuation of the assets or production of a balance sheet. Rather, the task is to examine the nature of the stream of cash flowing from individual assets or classes of

Figure 1: Main components of a government balance sheet

Assets	Liabilities
Cash invested[a]	Payments owing to suppliers
Accounts receivable	Borrowings outstanding[b]
Loans extended	Future stream of government spending on goods and services
Future stream of government taxes	
Equity invested in state-owned enterprises[c]	
Investment in infrastructural assets[d]	
Foreign exchange reserves held by the central bank	

a. Deposits at the central bank and in domestic bank accounts operated by government agencies; foreign currency liquidity invested by the debt office.

b. Short-term treasury bills and other government securities owned by the financial sector; government retail debt and foreign currency debt.

c. Includes ownership interests in the central bank and in government companies competing with the private sector. In some situations, this equity holding might be negative.

d. Commercial property and other forms of real estate (e.g., agricultural and forestry holdings, housing stock).

Figure 2: Simplified government balance sheet

Assets	Liabilities
Present value of stream of tax revenues	Present value of government outlays less debt servicing
	Market value of government debt

assets (such as loans, investments, and tax revenues) and to consider what might happen to these streams as interest rates and exchange rates change. It is best to begin by taking the largest, and dominant, asset in a government balance sheet—the tax and other revenues available to the government.

Figure 2 presents a highly simplified government balance sheet.

Balance sheet risk exists when there is a mismatch in the financial characteristics of assets and liabilities. Just as borrowing in yen to finance an investment (say, a house) creates balance sheet risk for an individual whose income is in dollars, so too for a company or a government. A government will have balance sheet risk when the financial characteristics of its debt vary significantly from the nature of the resources available to service it.

The balance sheets in figures 1 and 2 are only for illustrative purposes. It is not necessary to value the government's assets or derive present values. Rather, the objective should be to examine whether the cash flows associated with the assets and with government outlays can guide decisions on the type of debt that should be issued to finance government goods and services. In this context, debt could be regarded as equivalent to deferred taxation.

In many countries, the stream of government taxation revenue is received over a long period, and its magnitude is not appreciably affected by day-to-day movements in the exchange rate. Nor, for most countries, is the size of the revenue stream that the government expects to receive over the long run likely to be significantly correlated with real interest rate movements. Similarly, government expenditure flows are generally incurred in domestic currency and extend over a long period, and the scale of these flows is not greatly affected by movements in exchange rates or in real interest rates.

This suggests that the debt portfolio for most governments should consist of long-duration debt (reflecting the long-term nature of the revenue flows) and should be in domestic currency (since the revenue flows are not significantly affected by exchange rate movements). If the government's balance sheet is expected to be hit by significant demand shocks, it might also be prudent to place a portion of the debt in inflation-indexed instruments.

For most governments, this portfolio structure would result in much less balance sheet risk than would a portfolio of foreign currency debt, floating-rate debt, or short-maturity debt. This is a key reason why a central pillar of most government debt management strategies is to develop the domestic debt market and establish a yield curve in nominal fixed-rate debt instruments.

If the government's revenue stream is in foreign currency (e.g., if the government's revenues largely come from exporting commodities), the government should issue foreign currency debt in the same currency denomination as its revenues.

A government's balance sheet risk can be managed on a subportfolio basis. For example, foreign exchange reserves held at the central bank constitute another large financial asset owned by governments. Most governments divide these reserves into a liquidity portfolio, held in short-term or floating-rate securities and deposits, and an investment portfolio that is invested in longer-maturity assets that are expected to generate higher returns. A government's balance sheet risk would increase if it invested its foreign currency reserves in dollar deposits and financed the investment with long-dated borrowing in a different currency. The government would then have a currency and interest rate mismatch. Market risk associated with the government's foreign currency reserves could be minimized by matching the foreign currency and interest rate characteristics of the reserves with those of the foreign currency debt that funds it. This portfolio management approach is illustrated in figure 3.

The central bank should be free to decide (or to advise the minister of finance on) the desired currency composition and maturity of the foreign

Figure 3: Managing a balance sheet on a subportfolio basis

Assets	Liabilities

Market value of foreign exchange reserves
    Intervention portfolio
    Investment portfolio
	Market value of foreign currency debt
	    Deposits and short-term debt
	    Fixed-income instruments

Present value of stream of tax revenues.	Market-value of long-term, fixed-rate domestic currency debt
	Present value of stream of government outlays less debt servicing

exchange reserves. The debt office then would be responsible for ensuring that the government borrowing which funds these reserves matches as closely as possible the desired currency and interest rate characteristics of the foreign exchange reserves.

It may not be possible to achieve an exact match at all times between the currencies and interest rates of the foreign exchange reserves and of the debt used to finance these reserves. This is because the government's foreign exchange reserves will fluctuate depending on the nature of the exchange rate regime (that is, on whether the central bank provides a ready market for buying and selling foreign exchange) and the size of intervention and sterilization operations. Nevertheless, the main objective of reducing balance sheet risk can often be achieved by seeking to match-fund an average level of reserves, provided these are reasonably stable over time. If the reserve levels are extremely volatile, matching reserves and foreign currency debt may not be possible.

Cash flows associated with many of the remaining government assets are likely to be denominated in domestic currency and to be spread over a long period. In a project finance setting, these assets would be financed either by long-maturity, fixed-rate domestic currency debt or by price-indexed debt, depending on whether the cash flows are indexed to the rate of inflation. Equity investments—for example, in state-owned enterprises —have a long duration, and risk would be minimized by funding the assets in long-term, fixed-rate domestic currency debt. Other assets, such as national parks, government buildings, and roadways, may not generate marketable cash flows and are not directly relevant for this analysis. Nevertheless, the private sector often manages similar assets and sets prices for the output (e.g., road tolls, leases, and park entry fees). The way in which the private sector finances such assets could give some insight into what type of government debt should fund analogous assets, even though the government might not charge for the benefits flowing from them.

It is important to emphasize that this discussion of the risk characteristics of government assets does not mean that every government asset should be reviewed or its value assessed. Nor is it necessary to derive the present value of the government spending and revenue flows. But it is important, however, to consider the main classes of assets that the government owns, the possible life of the cash flows, and whether these flows are sensitive to changes in interest rates and exchange rates. Doing so can offer valuable insights into the desirable composition of the debt and ways of reducing financial risk on the government's balance sheet.

MANAGING GOVERNMENT BALANCE SHEET RISK WHEN THE DOMESTIC CAPITAL MARKET IS UNDERDEVELOPED

As has been seen, a portfolio of long-maturity, fixed-rate domestic currency debt (or a combination of fixed-rate and inflation-adjusted debt) is likely to be effective in reducing government balance sheet risk and in hedging the government's budgetary position against economic shocks. But, as discussed in chapters 2 and 9, many developing countries have only recently started building a government fixed-income market, while others have not yet begun. In these situations, the debt manager is often faced with issuing longer-maturity foreign currency debt, or short-term, floating-rate debt, or inflation-indexed domestic currency debt. In view of the low level of domestic savings in these economies and the need to avoid crowding out private sector borrowers or forcing them to borrow more expensive and riskier foreign currency debt, the government may decide to meet a large part of its financing needs by borrowing in foreign currency.

If the government has foreign currency reserves, or if a portion of its revenues are in foreign currency (e.g., from energy exports), a subportfolio of foreign currency debt can be used to match those foreign currency assets. If the remaining large government assets are in domestic currency, the government faces a currency mismatch. In this situation, the least-risk alternative is to find a portfolio of foreign currency debt that has the highest correlation with the domestic currency.

When the government has a credible fixed-exchange-rate peg, the least-risk approach would be to borrow in the currency or currencies making up the peg. A credible peg is likely to comprise the currency or currencies of the economy or economies with which the country is most closely integrated with respect to trade and capital flows. (Many Eastern European countries, for example, peg their currencies to the euro.)[4]

When the government has a floating exchange rate, statistical analysis can be used to find the least-risk currency choice—that is, the foreign currency or basket with the least volatility with respect to the domestic currency. This analysis should be undertaken using a long data series, if possible, and should be reviewed for robustness over shorter time periods. This is because the results can be affected by the economic policies in place, particularly those relating to the financial market. Structural adjustment reforms involving financial market deregulation and the opening of the capital account can markedly change the previous correlations.

If a long data series is unavailable, or if structural adjustment reforms have altered the previously existing relationships, an analysis of trade patterns and capital movements may give some insights into which currencies are likely to be most closely related to the value of the domestic currency. Even here, further refinement may be necessary if the country's main trading partners are in turn heavily trade-dependent on a major trading country such as the United States or a trading bloc such as the European Union. Borrowing in the currency of a neighboring country with which there is cross-border trade may be a poor choice, particularly if that country's financial markets are underdeveloped or heavily regulated.

If it is not possible to reach clear conclusions regarding trade or capital flows, the government might consider the type of approach outlined in chapter 7 for deriving a foreign currency benchmark. This might involve building up over time a foreign currency debt portfolio whose currency composition is based on another reference indicator such as relative global GDP weights or size of respective bond market capitalization.

Most developing country governments have net foreign currency debt. This reflects their needs as capital importers and their desire to maintain debt financed foreign currency reserves at a prudent level given their negative cost of carry. Even if a government has a credible exchange rate regime and is able to match the structure of the foreign exchange reserves and the debt underlying them, it still faces balance sheet risk. This is because the overall net debt flows and the financial resources needed to service them are likely to be in different currencies, and exchange rate regimes do not always remain credible under different stresses. Over the past 20 years, there have been several examples in Asia and Latin America of pegged exchange and crawling exchange rate regimes that could not be maintained when international capital flows became volatile. These examples highlight the importance of credible macroeconomic and structural adjustment policies in order to attract capital inflows that are invested in local currency denominated assets, and further illustrate the need for making the development of the domestic financial market an important policy priority.

NOTES

1. Similarly, the intermediary would have a risk exposure if its floating-rate borrowings and loans were repriced or reset on different days. This mismatch in the reset dates could be closed out by overlaying interest rate swaps on its borrowings.

2. Similarly, most individuals do not draw up a balance sheet, although they have financial assets and liabilities and a financial net worth at any point in time.

3. Equity in state-owned enterprises is often negative, and governments are faced with injecting additional capital. This measure is frequently accompanied by changes in the regulatory environment as a preliminary step toward privatization.

4. This does not, however, eliminate risk as there is always the possibility that the peg may fail.

Chapter 5

Developing a Risk Management Policy Framework

Risk management policies lie at the heart of government debt management, forming the critical link between the formulation and implementation of debt management strategy. Their development poses difficult, yet fundamental, choices for debt managers and policy makers. It requires the assessment of different types of risk, analysis of the trade off between expected cost and risk, and review of the way in which government debt management policy interacts with the instruments of macroeconomic policy, the management of foreign exchange reserves and the governance framework established for state-owned enterprises. Many of these issues are explored in other chapters of this book. This chapter discusses management and technical issues in developing risk management policies.

Prudent risk management policies that evolve in response to new risk analysis and better information on government risk preferences are essential for managing a government's balance sheet exposure and its ownership interests in the debt office. These policies establish limits on portfolio activities, identify the types of risk exposures acceptable to the government and, by directing the operations of the debt office, ensure consistency in the implementation of government debt management. Such policies are especially valuable when the debt office is experiencing high staff turnover.

Steps in setting up a risk management framework

The risk management process comprises several steps:

- Risk identification.
  Risk is a relative concept; it needs to be considered in relation to the objectives of the business or organization. Whether a particular invest-ment strategy is risky depends on the broader objectives or goals set for the organization. In the context of a government balance sheet, the risk surrounding the government's liabilities should be identified against the objectives of the assets being financed and the characteristics of the financial flows they generate.

- Risk analysis.
  Usually there is a trade off between expected cost (or expected returns) and the level of risk. Borrowers expect to pay higher debt servicing costs for longer maturity borrowings, or for issuing borrowing instruments which shift most of the risk to the investor. Similarly, investors expect lower returns for less risky investments. In a liability management con-text, risk analysis involves identifying and quantifying the costs and risks associated with a debt strategy and reviewing the portfolio combinations that reflect different cost/risk trade offs.

- Identifying a preferred strategy.
  In selecting a portfolio that best meets the issuer's tolerance for risk and expectations regarding cost, the objective is to find the most efficient strategy; that is, the one which has the lowest expected cost for an acceptable degree of risk. Usually, the selection of the preferred portfo-lio strategy is made by the minister of finance on the basis of advice received from the ministry of finance.[1]

- Implementing the debt strategy.
  The debt office is responsible for implementing the strategy, which can be represented by a strategic benchmark as discussed in chapter 7. With-in the debt office, the portfolio, risk management, payment, settlement and accounting activities will be governed by the risk management poli-cies and the procedures manuals in place. These policies should draw upon the risk analysis undertaken and in-house knowledge of sound debt management practices.

- Reporting performance and reviewing the strategy.
  Performance monitoring and reporting is usually undertaken within a middle office and typical activities include comparing the government's

borrowing costs in foreign currency with those achieved by other sovereign issuers; assessing the extent to which the portfolio differs from the strategic portfolio benchmark; and reporting the results of any tactical trading.[2]

The risk management framework should embrace the management of all aspects of market, credit and operational risk identified in table 1 in chapter 1. The next section describes issues relating to these risks.

MARKET RISK

Assets and liabilities change in value when their projected cash flows are sensitive to movements in relative prices such as interest rates, exchange rates and commodity prices. Changes in market prices affect the value of the benchmark portfolio as well as the actual portfolio, and accordingly the size of the portfolio correction needed to bring the actual portfolio closer to the benchmark.

Market risk is managed by identifying the preferred currency composition and duration of the debt portfolio and formulating decision rules for transactions to move the actual portfolio closer to the strategic benchmarks over time. (Currency and duration benchmarks are often expressed in terms of a range or band.) Questions as to whether tactical trading should be permitted need to be examined; if such trading is undertaken, position limits and loss limits need to be established.

Market risk is usually calculated with financial models. These range from relatively simple scenario based models to complex software using highly sophisticated statistical and simulation techniques. For countries just beginning to model portfolio risk, it is often best to start with less complex models and build additional complexity as understanding increases. Provided that the risks have been identified accurately and the model is well specified to capture those risks, such models can adequately estimate the costs and risks of alternative strategies and rank them on the basis of their cost/risk or risk/reward trade offs.

Modeling approaches used within debt offices to capture the long term impact of market risk and help identify a benchmark portfolio, are often based on "cost at risk" or "budget at risk" techniques. These models attempt to measure the extent to which the government's debt servicing costs, and hence its budget outlays, would be affected by an increase in interest rates. For example, the "cost at risk" analyses could indicate with a

95% probability that the debt servicing costs for the following year will not exceed a certain level, measured in local currency.

Cost-at-risk models simulate debt-servicing flows for the existing debt portfolio and the new debt expected to be issued under different possible debt strategies. These strategies might include various combinations of domestic and foreign currency debt, changing proportions of fixed rate and floating rate debt, and varying maturities. Typically, a Monte Carlo process is used to generate a large number of interest rate and exchange rate scenarios that provide a basis for setting up probability distributions of future debt servicing costs. These relative price projections (which may be for as long as 10 years) can be applied to the range of debt-servicing flows and the forecast revenue available to service the government's debt. Market risk can be measured by the extent to which the time path of debt servicing flows diverge from or converge on the revenues available to service the debt.

However, cost-at-risk models can have important limitations. Cost-at-risk calculations are often very sensitive to the assumptions made and, accordingly, are often used to supplement information on duration and average time to maturity in determining a preferred portfolio structure. Furthermore, in order to calculate meaningful cost-at-risk figures, a historical series of market-generated interest rates and exchange rates is required. Because many developing countries lack this, a simple scenario analysis is often more appropriate.

Should government debt managers trade on the basis of personal views?

Several experiences during the 1980s and 1990s demonstrate how poor management of asset and liability portfolios can lead to large financial losses for shareholders and taxpayers. Examples include the failure of Barings Bank (1995), large trading losses by Metallgesellschaft (1993), Procter and Gamble (1994), Daiwa Bank (1995), Morgon Grenfell (1996), the near failure of Long Term Capital Management (1998), and the $153 billion of losses generated by the savings and loans industry in the United States between 1986 and 1995, and the losses associated with structured investments entered into by Orange County in the United States (1994). These instances often involved taking views on interest rates (U.S. savings and loan industry, Orange County, Daiwa bank, Long Term Capital Management, Procter and Gamble), exchange rates (Long Term Capital Management), equity prices (Barings bank, Morgan Grenfell) and commodity

prices (Metallgesellschaft). These losses often arose from or were exacer-
bated by a serious breakdown in operational procedures. In the light of
these experiences, an important question is whether government debt managers should trade tactically based on personal views about interest rates
and exchange rates.

Every government managing a debt portfolio should decide the basis on
which it wants its debt managers to form expectations of future movements
in interest rates and exchange rates. One approach, based on the efficient
market hypothesis, suggests that the best predictor of interest rates is the
forward rates embedded in current yield curves and that future exchange
rate movements are implied by the interest rate differentials between countries. Although actual prices may differ substantially from those suggested
by market forward curves, forward prices are considered to be "an un-
biased" forecast of exchange rates and interest rates.

An alternative approach is to assume that forward curves are not an efficient predictor of future prices and that government debt managers are better able to predict relative prices. If this were the case, government debt
managers would be able to use their forecasts to lower the government's
debt servicing costs and reduce risk. In order to achieve this, government
debt managers would require information or analytical techniques that
are superior to other market participants, and must be able to transact
efficiently. The first criteria provides an extremely difficult challenge for a
government debt manager, especially one transacting in foreign capital
markets. In these markets, government debt managers generally have little
or no information of their own on the nature of the financial flows. They
do not have direct access to the sources of information on currency flows
that the large global commercial and investment banks have, nor do they
have the resources to develop superior quantitative techniques.[3]

Government debt managers usually have more information on financial
flows in their domestic market. However, for several reasons, most governments consider it unwise to tactically trade in this market in an attempt
to make profits. The government is usually the dominant issuer of bonds
in the domestic market, and the government would risk being accused of
manipulating the market or using inside information of a regulatory and
budgetary nature if it became a market maker or trader in government
bonds for the purposes of trying to generate additional income. If it took
currency or interest rate positions, its actions might be interpreted as signaling a government view on the desired direction of the exchange rate and
interest rates, making the central bank's task more difficult.

These types of tactical transactions differ from the strategic portfolio transactions debt managers often undertake in the domestic bond market aimed at meeting the government's duration objectives or increasing market liquidity for investors. For example, in several countries, government debt managers transact interest rate swaps in their domestic market in order to modify the duration or interest rate sensitivity of the government's domestic debt portfolio. They also announce offers to buy-back illiquid issues of government bonds or replace them with more liquid government maturities.

A few countries (for example, Austria, Ireland, New Zealand and Sweden) permit their government debt managers to tactically trade a portion of the governments foreign-currency liquidity. They do so for a variety of reasons, including trying to exploit market imperfections or market mispricing in an attempt to generate profits or reduce the cost of the debt portfolio without significantly altering its risk profile; and increasing the market experience of the portfolio managers in an attempt to achieve cost savings on future strategic transactions such as major borrowings. If tactical trading is permitted, it should comprise only a small fraction of a government's portfolio management activities, and be executed under clearly defined portfolio guidelines covering position and loss limits, compliance procedures and performance reporting. Position limits can be derived using a value-at-risk framework based on analysis of how large a loss could be expected at various statistical levels of confidence (expressed in terms of standard deviations). Loss limits are frequently expressed as the maximum financial loss that is permissible over a specific period of time (e.g., one month) before a position is closed out (and, possibly, all tactical trading ceases for a specified period).

Assessing the effectiveness of tactical trading is particularly important and the Swedish National Debt Office (SNDO) has developed a very useful method for this. Since 1992, the SNDO has allocated part of its tactical trading limit to external managers under the same guidelines that apply to its own portfolio managers. External managers undertake liability management trades within carefully defined limits with the objective of trying to lower the overall cost of the government's debt portfolio. Their tactical trading performance is constantly monitored and compared with that of the SNDO managers.

Most governments, however, do not permit their debt managers to undertake tactical trading. They believe that it represents a poor use of taxpayers resources because it is unlikely to generate positive risk-adjusted returns and creates unnecessary balance sheet risk for a government.

Should governments hedge their asset and liability positions?

Governments should look for natural hedges in their asset and liability portfolios which enable them to reduce risk on the government's balance sheet and lower transaction costs. Natural hedges occur when the portfolio exposures can be structured to offset one another without recourse to purchasing financial derivatives. As discussed in chapter 4, a natural hedge can be constructed by ensuring that the currency and interest rate composition of government borrowing used to finance a government's foreign exchange reserves matches as closely as possible the currency and interest rate structure of the reserves.

After natural hedges have been established, governments who have access to financial derivatives then need to decide whether to purchase them in order to construct financial hedges and reduce market risk. In the private sector, these decisions are often relatively straightforward and are driven by objectives of reducing expected taxes, lowering the risk of bankruptcy, increasing borrowing capacity and lowering borrowing costs.[4] Like the private sector, governments should decide whether to construct financial hedges on the basis of the expected benefits of reducing financial risk, taking into account the transaction costs and incremental credit risks involved. Where these transaction costs and credit risks are acceptable, governments generally prefer to hedge their exposures given their preferences for greater certainty and less cash flow volatility.

Hedging costs are important in deciding which market risks to hedge. For example, even if a country with a large foreign-currency portfolio could purchase an option providing protection against currency depreciation, it would be extremely expensive. This is because exchange rate volatility in the past may have been high, country credit risk may be substantial and the hedge providers know that the government, through its macroeconomic and structural adjustment polices, is able to influence the exchange rate in the short term.

Country creditworthiness considerations frequently prevent developing countries from accessing hedging products. Some of the multilateral development banks have responded to this by intermediating hedging transactions and passing the terms on to their developing country client. The introduction of the World Bank's new loan and hedging products in 2000, for example, enables IBRD borrowers to hedge their existing IBRD loans on similar terms to a AAA-rated institution, and to obtain hedges embedded in Libor based fixed spread loans.[5]

Even when IBRD borrowers have access to hedging instruments, government debt managers are sometimes reluctant to use them. Adequate debt recording and accounting systems may not be in place, and the debt managers may not wish to be held accountable for decisions that differ from their predecessors. What is often not fully appreciated in the latter situation however, is that hedging instruments can be a valuable tool for managing financial risk. A decision not to hedge leaves the portfolio vulnerable to market risk and could affect the governments debt servicing commitments.

REFINANCING OR ROLLOVER RISK

Measures include specifying the acceptable maturity profile of the portfolio and the degree of refinancing risk in a single year. Policies may, for example, limit the amount of debt maturing in any one year or seek to reduce portfolio concentration of short-term debt by establishing maximum ratios of short-term or floating-rate debt to total government debt. Currencies and instruments in which the debt office can transact also need to be identified.

LIQUIDITY RISK

Liquidity risk is dealt with through liquidity management policies that normally specify minimum levels of foreign currency liquidity, the instruments and currencies in which this liquidity can be held, and a portfolio benchmark for investing the liquidity. The policies might, for example, establish prudent minimum levels of liquidity, such as requiring the debt office to maintain foreign currency liquidity levels equivalent to the subsequent six months of foreign currency debt servicing. They might specify that part of this liquidity must be invested in highly liquid instruments, while another portion can be invested in instruments that have a longer duration or that are less liquid. Liquidity levels may need to be established for a domestic currency debt portfolio if the government believes that it may not be able to borrow readily from the market in its own currency. This can be the case when domestic capital markets lack depth.

CREDIT RISK

Decisions on how much credit exposure to accept on the investment side will depend on the government's tolerance for risk and the size of the negative cost of carry it is prepared to accept. The latter reflects the differences between the cost of funding and the expected investment returns.

Credit risk is managed using policies that establish limits on the government's credit exposure to individual counterparties through swap transactions or the investment of liquid assets. Acceptable limits for credit exposure are often based on the credit ratings assigned by the sovereign credit rating institutions and on the marked-to-market exposure of the position, the type of instrument involved, and the time to maturity. Limits should be discussed with the officials responsible for managing the government's foreign exchange reserves so that the desirable level of credit exposure can be assessed in the context of a broader component of the government's balance sheet rather than for the debt portfolio in isolation. Sublimits for specific transactions, such as swaps, may also be needed. For example, sublimits for swaps could specify exposure limits for different counterparty credit ratings at which agreed types of collateral have to be posted. The policy may also include requirements to close out swap positions if a counterparty credit rating falls below a certain level. Credit risk around swap transactions can also be reduced by using standardized master derivatives agreements and arrangements for netting and posting collateral.[6]

In deciding who are acceptable counterparties, central banks and debt offices should be guided by the longitudinal histories of default probabilities that are maintained by the sovereign credit rating agencies. These show the extent to which rated entities migrate to lower ratings or default over time. Not surprisely, the longitudinal ratings migration matrices indicate that the probability of default by AA and AAA rated financial institutions is extremely low over the short run. Restricting the list of eligible investment instruments or counterparties for debt office transactions may reduce expected returns and increase carrying costs, but by helping mitigate credit risk, it lessens the possibility of substantial balance sheet losses.

Some central banks and debt offices in emerging markets place deposits with local banks that have poor credit ratings. In doing so, these institutions are increasing their credit risk and the potential for moral hazard, in that the local intermediary may believe there is a strong possibility of government support if it experiences financial difficulty and may consequently take greater balance sheet risk.

The initiatives above can significantly reduce the magnitude of the credit risk facing a government. Still, loss of income through counterparty default can be a sensitive issue, particularly if a review concludes that the loss could have been avoided had more prudent limits been adopted or more rigorous credit analysis been undertaken. Such a conclusion would damage the reputation of the government and its debt managers.

SETTLEMENT RISK

Measures to manage settlement risk include requirements to select suitable settlement banks, custodians, clearing brokers, and fiscal agents and to decide the maximum amount of exposure to any one settlement institution. Settlement payments on debt management transactions can be extremely large, and settlement failures can involve substantial interest rate expense. Settlement policies may also provide for overdraft facilities with settlement banks and specify a financial limit for them.[7] Settlement procedures that deal with the preparation, checking, and authorization of debt-servicing payments and transfers between bank accounts are also critical.

OPERATIONAL RISK

Operational risk is managed through policies concerned with mitigating business risks that could threaten the continuity and the reputation of the treasury operation. Such policies should outline management and group responsibilities and identify controls and procedures for managing transactions and associated payment flows.[8]

Operational risk can be reduced by introducing the types of governance practices discussed in chapter 3 and the systems management principles outlined in chapter 7. These elements include sound and transparent debt management objectives, well defined responsibilities and clear delegations, systems of internal checks and balances supported by an efficient organizational structure, sound information technology management, quality assurance (provided through an advisory board or oversight committee, external auditors, and outside reviews by independent consultants), and timely and focused reporting to the minister of finance and the parliament.

The severity of risk depends on several considerations, including the effectiveness of the governance framework, the robustness of the debt management strategy and risk management framework, and the quality of staffing and information systems. Gains and losses from active portfolio trading are unlikely to be material in the leading debt offices, which tend to have well-developed debt management strategies, conservative position and loss limits, and effective monitoring and control procedures.

Often, the main day-to-day operational risk stems from shortcomings in business processes and human resource policies. A common challenge here is to decrease keyperson risk within the organization and reduce the multiplicity of tasks carried out by experienced staff, while at the same time eliminating duplication of functions within the organization.

The most common operational risks tend to lie on the transaction side (e.g., errors in confirming and settling trades), but the most serious ones generally relate to fraudulent breaches of controls and systems failure. Each carries a serious financial and reputational cost. Even with comprehensive management controls, it is always possible for a limited number of people, through collaboration, to attempt to defraud the government by diverting a settlement payment, since there may be a day's delay before the counterparty inquires about the settlement failure. This is why a sound risk management culture, well-defined controls and quality assurance practices, and separate reporting lines are so important.

Disasters represent another form of operational risk. The terrorist attack on New York City's World Trade Center in September 2001 led to a renewed international focus on the vulnerability of businesses to disasters and a heightened emphasis on business continuity procedures. Many debt offices and central banks have reviewed their needs for alternative backup sites and data storage facilities.

NOTES

1. Where a debt office has been established outside the ministry of finance, the advice might be provided jointly by the ministry of finance and the debt office.

2. Cost comparisons of foreign currency borrowing are often approximate. The borrowing spread over the government curve is usually public information, but the cost relative to Libor, or a related pricing benchmark, will be an estimate given that the terms of any swap transaction (if the

issuer's goal say is to obtain floating rate funding in a preferred currency) will remain confidential between the issuer and the swap counterparty.

3. The analytical and information processing difficulties facing government debt managers in predicting market price movements in these markets are considerable. Daily turnover in the foreign exchange market for example is around US$1.5 trillion.

4. See for example, Smith, C.W. Jr., Smithson, C.W., Wilord, D.S., *Five Reasons Why Companies should Manage Risk*, in Schwartz, R.J. and Smith, C.W. Jr., *The Handbook of Currency and Interest Rate Risk Management*. New York Institute of Finance, 1990.

5. The World Bank introduced LIBOR based fixed spread loans which enable IBRD borrowers to customize amortization terms and manage currency and interest rate risk over the life of the loan through a range of loan conversion options (for example, borrowers can change the currency composition and interest rate basis of disbursed cash flows). The stand-alone hedging products enable borrowers to enter into currency and interest rate swaps, interest rate caps and collars and commodity hedges with the Bank. Similar hedging products are available through the European Bank for Reconstruction and Development and the International Finance Corporation.

6. Most standard swap documentation includes provision for netting exposure.

7. The overdraft facility may cover situations in which, because of timing mismatches, the funds may be a few hours late in arriving but the loan agreements specify that foreign currency debt-servicing payments must be made early in the business day.

8. For example, the portfolio policy might specify the legal authorities for debt management and be cross-referenced to the subdelegation of responsibilities.

Chapter 6

Contingent Liabilities in a Government Asset-and-Liability Management Framework

Contingent liabilities represent potential financial claims against the government that have not yet materialized but that could trigger a firm financial obligation or liability under certain circumstances. There are two main types: explicit and implicit.

Explicit contingent liabilities are based on a contractual commitment or a formal acknowledgment of a potential claim that may become active in particular situations. These liabilities may include bonds or other instruments with put option features issued by the government; credit-related and performance-related guarantees; various government insurance schemes (e.g., against crop failure or natural disasters); and legal proceedings representing claims against government providers of services such as health care, education, defense, and housing.

Implicit contingent liabilities arise when, even though the government does not have a contractual obligation to provide financial support, society expects the government to provide assistance because of moral considerations or because the opportunity cost of not intervening is considered to be unacceptable. These liabilities could include disaster relief, corporate sector bailouts, municipal bankruptcies, and defaults on nonguaranteed debt issued by subnational governments and state-owned enterprises (Polackova 1998).

Implicit contingent liabilities can often generate large government debt obligations, especially when government policy signals have created incentives for greater risk taking. This was particularly true in East Asia in the late 1990s. The balance sheets of banks and corporations in many East Asian countries contained large asset and liability mismatches, which stemmed in part from the perception that the government had made an irreversible commitment to defend the exchange rate peg. Institutions, judging that their currency risk was negligible, borrowed in foreign currency and lent in domestic currency or in a different foreign currency to generate higher-interest-rate returns. In the aftermath of their currency devaluations, governments in the region recognized that many of these financial institutions were insolvent and that the demands for large-scale recapitalization of institutions represented a major implicit liability.

Excessive risk taking by financial intermediaries can also occur if the prudential supervisory framework is inadequate, especially when new opportunities are arising as a result of financial sector deregulation and capital account liberalization. The added systemic risk can substantially increase a government's implicit contingent obligations.

Governments are often attracted to contractual arrangements resulting in contingent liabilities because they attach a low probability to the contingent liability being exercised and because of budgetary accounting rules. Under conventional budget rules, loan guarantees and other contingent liabilities are often not recognized in the budget until they are triggered. In addition, fees generated for providing the guarantees are recognized as current receipts in the budget.

Several studies have shown that once contingent liabilities have materialized, they can be a major factor in the buildup of public sector debt. Particularly important in this regard have been contingent liabilities that resulted in capital injections into the banking system or in the recapitalization of public sector enterprises. For example, table 7 suggests that government capital injections into the banking systems in some East Asian countries implied a very large increase in government debt. In Korea and Thailand these financial demands more than doubled the share of public debt in relation to GDP.

Contingent liabilities can be very large in developed countries, as in the cases of the U.S. government's fiscal support for the savings and loan industry in the 1980s and the financial assistance that Norway and Sweden extended to their banking sectors in the early 1990s. In both instances, the governments intervened beyond their contractual obligations. In emerging

Table 7: Public debt and banking sector recapitalization costs as a share of GDP, 1998
   (*percent*)

	Indonesia[a]	Malaysia	Korea, Rep. of	Thailand
Public debt	72.5	33.3	10.5	14.6
Estimated recapitalization costs	58.3	10.0	16.0	31.9
Estimated debt after recapitalization	106.6	43.3	26.5	46.6

a. 1997 data are used for Indonesia.
Source: World Bank 2000b.

markets, government contingent liabilities can be particularly large in relation to GDP or to government budgetary aggregates. Many of these governments are in the process of privatizing their infrastructures or are seeking private sector participation in new infrastructure development. These policy goals have frequently been accompanied by requests from the private sector for guarantees or, in the case of privatization, for assumption by the government of the debts of state-owned enterprises prior to their sale.

MANAGING RISK ASSOCIATED WITH CONTINGENT LIABILITIES

Contingent liabilities represent a substantial balance sheet risk for a government and are a potential source of future tax rate variability. Their magnitude is shaped by the same types of macroeconomic and financial risk that affect the government's other liabilities. Unlike most government financial obligations, contingent liabilities have option-type characteristics in that (a) the contingent obligation can be exercised only if certain events occur and (b) the size of the fiscal payout may depend on a strike price (e.g., if the obligation relates to a guaranteed minimum market price for a commodity).

If a bank issued such a contingent liability, it would endeavor to assess the value of the obligations it had entered into and would price them on the basis of their risk characteristics. As part of its balance sheet management, it would make provision for expected losses against its annual income and would hold capital against the risk of unexpected losses. Clients would be charged a guarantee fee based on the guarantor's cost of borrowing plus the costs incurred by the guarantor in provisioning and in building up reserves against unanticipated losses.

Governments can introduce many public policy measures to contain the risk of contingent liabilities. Important first steps are to decide on the preferred risk exposure, to review the explicit contingent liabilities the government has entered into, and to establish policy criteria for evaluating all new requests for guarantees and underwriting commitments. A government should decide whether and under what circumstances it might be prepared to accept financial liability for the performance of state-owned enterprises or private sector entities. It is also important to disclose, in the most transparent way possible, the nature and extent of the government's explicit contingent liabilities and who the potential beneficiaries are.[1] Because contingent liabilities, like regulations, are often viewed by governments as an inexpensive means of achieving policy goals and a way to reduce budgetary outlays, the expected budgetary impact of existing and new contingent liabilities should be fully disclosed in the government's budget documentation. In its Code of Good Practices on Fiscal Transparency, for example, the IMF recommends that countries disclose in their budget documentation the main contingent liabilities of the central government, briefly describe their nature, and indicate the potential beneficiaries. Best practice, as recommended by the code, would call for governments to provide an estimate of the expected cost of each contingent liability, wherever possible, and to explain the basis for the estimate.

Risk-sharing mechanisms should be included in the design of contingent liabilities to ensure that the situations that could trigger the contingent liability are not under the control of the beneficiaries. Were the opposite the case, it would create moral hazard risks for the government if the beneficiaries became less risk averse or more opportunistic in their behavior. Sound risk-sharing arrangements involve providing termination dates for contingent claims; pricing contingent liabilities on a risk-adjusted basis and charging the beneficiaries accordingly; requiring beneficiaries to post collateral; and breaking down blanket risk guarantees into their discrete risk dimensions so that risk can be more evenly distributed between the government and the potential beneficiaries.

Promoting sound governance arrangements for managing subnational entities and state-owned enterprises, and making them accountable for managing their own risks, would also help reduce the risks associated with contingent liabilities. Because managers in state-owned enterprises do not face takeover risk unless the organization is to be privatized, careful consideration should be given to the design of incentive structures and sanctions to induce the desired managerial performance. Similarly, initiatives to shape the incentive framework for subnational enterprises may be needed to improve performance and reduce the risk that these bodies will require financial assistance in the future.

Improvement of the quality of the government's economic management can also help reduce the risk that contingent liabilities will be realized. Valuable measures in this regard include establishing prudent macroeconomic policies and improving the supervision and regulation of the banking system, using such provisions as mandatory risk limits and minimum capital requirements. Sound accounting and disclosure requirements for private and state-owned entities are important mechanisms for reducing the risk of a systemic crisis and should help limit the government's exposure if a crisis occurs.

Experience in many countries, such as Colombia, Hungary, New Zealand, South Africa, and Sweden, suggests that more complete disclosure, better risk-sharing arrangements, improved governance structures for state-owned entities, and sound economic policies can substantially reduce the government's exposure to contingent liabilities.

CONTINGENT LIABILITIES AND THE GOVERNMENT DEBT MANAGER

Debt managers in public sector enterprises sometimes create contingent liabilities for the government by issuing debt with put options in an attempt to lower debt-servicing costs. These options can create considerable risk for the government because they are often triggered in special circumstances such as a credit rating downgrade. For example, in 1997 the Industrial Finance Corporation of Thailand issued bonds with put options that could be exercised by the investor if the corporation were downgraded. In Mexico in 1998, Petróleos Mexicanos, the government-owned oil company, issued puttable bonds that could have been sold back to the issuer if the issuer were downgraded.[2]

As the contagion from the 1997–98 Asian financial crisis indicated, the events that trigger rating downgrades and make market access difficult need not be country or company specific. By writing put options, the issuer risks having to go to the market to refinance debt at a time when market access may be difficult for emerging market borrowers and spreads are substantially wider. This was the case in Argentina, Brazil, and Mexico in 1999, when a number of corporate bodies had large, deep-in-the-money puttable bonds that fell due in 1999.[3] In general, governments and state-owned entities should be very careful about issuing puttable bonds.

Historically, government debt managers have played only a small role in managing the risks associated with contingent liabilities. Contingent obligations were often not disclosed by the government, and government debt managers frequently became aware of their existence only when the contingent claim was triggered and additional borrowing was needed. These days, debt managers' involvement may include raising funds (often from international capital markets, given the magnitude of the borrowing and the immediacy of the need), valuing contingent exposures, and providing advice on balance sheet restructuring of underperforming state entities. They also discuss with the sovereign credit rating agencies the extent of the government's exposure to contingent liabilities and the government's policy with respect to possible balance sheet support to entities in the event of potential insolvency.

The expansion of contingent liabilities can have important implications for future fiscal adjustment (for example, in deciding whether to increase taxation or borrowing and whether to cut spending). It is therefore desirable that a central government agency take the responsibility for monitoring the risk exposures that the government is entering into through its explicit contingent liabilities; for ensuring that the government is well informed of these risks; and for evaluating new and existing risk-covering instruments in order to standardize budgetary procedures and better control the fiscal impact of the liabilities.

Many countries now assign to the ministry of finance responsibility for monitoring the government's explicit contingent liabilities and designing contingent-based instruments. Some, such as Colombia and Sweden, pass this responsibility on to the government debt manager.[4] The reason is that much of the central government's risk management expertise lies with government debt managers, who are assumed to have a good understanding of the government's balance sheet risk. As discussed in chapter 3, some government debt offices are now being organized so that they can focus more sharply on the government's balance sheet risk. In addition, some governments have adopted committee structures that bring together the government's fiscal advisers, liability managers, and individuals responsible for managing some of the larger government-owned assets.

Best practice would be to price all guarantees and contingent liabilities on a risk-adjusted basis while including provisions for expected losses in the government's budget (see Currie and Velandia 1999). Most governments rely on their capacity to tax and borrow, and on their holdings of foreign exchange reserves, in order to meet unexpected financial claims.

Government debt managers could take responsibility for advising the minister of finance on the design of contingent liabilities and for making recommendations to the government on appropriate provisioning. Where risk-adjusted pricing is possible, the revenue from the risk premium would enable these reserves to be built up over time. The government may want to consider allocating some initial capital to these reserves in the event that a contingent liability is called prior to the reserves' being adequately built up through fee income. The amount of capital allocated would reflect the government's risk preferences. If it is not possible to quantify the cost and risk of the explicit contingent liabilities, the available information could be summarized in notes to the budget tables or to the government's financial accounts.

What is possible in this area depends on the quality of the risk management skills available to the government and the quality of the systems technology available for assessing risk; the quality of the governance arrangements for state-owned enterprises and state and local governments; the degree to which state-owned enterprises are well managed and decentralized; and the enterprises' technical capacity for risk management. If the necessary skills are not available within the government, external expertise should be contracted, and development of capacity within government to undertake these functions should become a policy objective.

NOTES

1. It should be noted that disclosure of *implicit* contingent liabilities could result in greater moral hazard costs for the government if the private sector views this disclosure as a commitment or as an indication that the government is likely to provide future financial assistance.

2. Because the put may be exercisable by the holder if the issuer is downgraded, the premium received by the issuer is likely to be reduced by the default risk that the market prices into the bond.

3. When the option is deep in the money, the issuer expects to have to buy back the bonds (when the option expires) at a price considerably above the current market price.

4. The Swedish National Debt Office is the only Swedish government agency that can issue government guarantees. The office has developed a model for pricing guarantees in which clients are charged a risk-based premium and all revenues and losses are met from a fund that is separate from the budget. In Colombia, the General Directorate of Public Credit is developing a methodology for valuing contingent liabilities on the basis of Monte Carlo simulations. It plans to use this methodology to evaluate the risks associated with a wide range of government guarantees and to establish clear budgetary procedures for disclosure and provisioning.

Chapter 7

The Use of Strategic Benchmarks in Government Asset-and-Liability Management

A strategic benchmark represents the desired structure or composition of a liability portfolio in terms of characteristics such as currency and interest rate mix and overall maturity. It is a powerful management tool because it forces a government to evaluate its risk tolerance and clarify its portfolio preferences in the face of what are often conflicting objectives regarding expected cost, market risk, and refinancing and liquidity risk. However, strategic benchmarks can be very damaging if poorly specified and applied. This chapter describes the value of strategic benchmarks in helping governments manage their liability portfolios and examines important issues in the design and implementation of these benchmarks.

DEFINITION OF STRATEGIC BENCHMARKS

A benchmark, generally speaking, refers to a reference for measurement or simply a point of reference. A stock market index, for example, can serve as a benchmark for assessing the performance of an equity portfolio, and the government yield curve is often referred to as the benchmark or reference for pricing public and private sector fixed-income securities.

A strategic benchmark represents the portfolio structure that the government would prefer to have for its debt portfolio. This preferred portfolio structure is not based on views about relative prices but instead reflects the government's preference as to the tradeoff between expected cost and risk. Accordingly, a strategic benchmark is considered to be market neutral in that it does not reflect any views of the government or its debt managers about the possible future market direction of exchange rates and interest rates.

Strategic benchmarks for a government debt portfolio are often expressed as minimum and maximum levels of acceptable risk exposure. For example, they may specify:

- Acceptable interest rate risk for the overall debt portfolio. This is usually based on a target level, or a range, for duration of the borrowing and may include the desired proportions of fixed-rate and floating-rate debt in the portfolio.

- The desired currency composition of the portfolio, including the proportion of domestic and foreign currency debt and the currency composition within the foreign currency debt portfolio.

- The debt maturity profile or the acceptable level of refinancing risk for the portfolio. A limit on the amount of debt maturing at any time is usually established on the basis of a quantifiable ceiling or expressed as a percentage of the overall portfolio.

Strategic benchmarks should, ideally, be derived for the overall debt portfolio, as the tradeoff between expected cost and risk often arises from the choice between long-term fixed-rate foreign-currency borrowing and short-term domestic-currency borrowing. Separate strategic benchmarks are, however, commonly adopted for the domestic currency and foreign currency debt portfolios.

Foreign currency benchmarks should preferably be derived for a government's net foreign currency debt portfolio rather than its gross foreign currency debt. As discussed in chapter 4, whenever possible, part of the gross foreign currency debt should be matched against the currency and interest rate structure of the government's foreign currency reserves in order to reduce the government's overall currency and interest rate risk.[1] This is particularly desirable with respect to the investment portfolio of the foreign exchange reserves. It may be more difficult to achieve in the intervention portfolio. Matching frees government debt managers to concentrate their risk management activities on the government's remaining net foreign currency exposure.

If it is not possible to set a liability benchmark that matches all or part of the government's foreign currency reserves, government debt managers should ensure that any foreign currency liquidity portfolio they manage is included in the construction of strategic benchmarks. It would make little sense, for example, to increase the government's balance sheet risk by investing the foreign currency liquidity managed by the government debt managers in yen if the government's foreign currency debt is in dollars.

Table 8 shows strategic government debt management benchmarks that have been established in various countries.

THE ROLE OF STRATEGIC BENCHMARKS

Strategic benchmarks constitute a valuable building block of government asset and liability management. They guide decisionmaking regarding tradeoffs between expected costs and risks, provide a framework for assessing portfolio performance, and enable continuity of policy direction. These roles are summarized briefly here.

Guidance for management of costs and risks

The task of deriving an appropriate strategic benchmark for a government debt portfolio, with the goal of lowering expected cost or reducing risk in the government balance sheet, is considerably more difficult than the benchmark challenges faced by asset fund managers, corporations, and financial intermediaries. The balance sheet setting in which the latter portfolios are managed is much more precise than is the case for government debt management. For example, an asset fund manager only works with one side of the book, the asset side, and does not need to worry about the cost of funds. The benchmark against which the asset fund manager manages the portfolio (say, an equity or fixed-income index) can be viewed as representing the liability structure of the balance sheet. The fund manager's task is clear: to outperform the market index. Banks, corporate treasuries, and insurance companies usually have well-defined business goals and a set of financial assets, which provide a natural reference point for managing risk in the debt portfolio and a basis for constructing liability benchmarks. For example, if a bank's liability structure consists of deposits from local investors, it will reduce its overall balance sheet risk by investing in a portfolio of local currency assets with an overall duration similar to that of its deposits.

Government debt managers have a less complete balance sheet to work with than do their private sector counterparts. As discussed in chapter 4, however, it is possible to develop government debt benchmarks that can

Table 8: Structure of strategic benchmarks, selected countries

Country (and date)	Ratio of domestic to foreign currency	Domestic (D) or foreign (F) currency benchmark	Ratio of fixed-rate to floating-rate debt	Modified duration (years)	Maximum refinancing ceilings and refinancing guidelines
Australia (8/2002)	100:0[a]	D	—	3 ± 0.5	—
Belgium (7/2003)	98:2–100:0[b]	D	—	3.9 ± 0.3	10–15% on debt maturing in next year; smooth redemption profile; weighted average maturity, 6.2 ± 0.1 years
Colombia (12/2001)	67:33	F	70:30	3.5	15% in 12 months, 30% in 36 months
Denmark (3/2003)	88:12[c]	D + F	—	3.5 ± 0.5	Smooth redemption profile of total debt
France (12/2001)	100:0	D	10% in inflation-indexed debt	—	Average maturity of 5.5 years
Ireland (6/2003)	98:2–100.0	D	—	3.7	—
Italy (12/2001)	75:25	D	75:25	3.5	Increase average life and smooth redemption profile
New Zealand (6/2003)	100:0[d]	D	80:20–70:30	—	Maintain an even maturity profile

114

Portugal (3/2003)	100:0	D	68:32	3.0	20% in 12 months, 35% in 24 months, 45% in 36 months
Sweden (9/2002)[e]	73:27[f]	D F	—	2.7 ± 0.3 2.3 ± 0.3	25% in 12 months; maintain a dispersed maturity profile
United Kingdom (7/2003)	100:0[d]	D			Issue a variety of debt instruments
United States (8/2003)	100:0	D	—		Issue securities across a wide range of maturities

— Not applicable.

a. In September 2001, the treasurer instructed the Australian Office of Financial Management (AOFM) to begin a program for orderly elimination of foreign currency exposure on a schedule agreed between the AOFM, the Treasury, and the Reserve Bank of Australia and concluding no later than 2008.

b. The government's policy is to repay its foreign currency debt in full as soon as possible.

c. The norm for domestic borrowing states that the issuance of domestic krone-denominated government securities within a year shall match the gross central government borrowing requirement less redemptions of foreign debt. The norm for foreign borrowing states that the central government's redemptions of foreign debt are to be refinanced by foreign borrowing.

d. Foreign debt is incurred only to finance international reserves; hence, there is zero net foreign currency debt.

e. The benchmark, to be achieved by 2004, covers only nominal debt and does not include inflation-indexed debt. The long-term goal is to reduce the proportion of foreign currency debt and increase the share of domestic currency inflation-indexed debt.

f. The long-term aim is a reduction in the foreign currency debt as a percentage of total central government debt and an increase in the percentage of krona-denominated debt.

Source: National debt offices.

reduce the government's balance sheet risk by taking into account the risk characteristics of the main cash flows that are available for servicing the government's debt. This usually involves finding a currency composition for the government's foreign currency debt that has a low variance (or as little variance as possible) with the domestic currency, since the government's tax revenues—the largest asset on its balance sheet, and the asset drawn on to repay and service creditors—is usually denominated in domestic currency. If the government's tax revenue is mainly denominated in a particular foreign currency (which can be the case, for example, if the government is a large commodity exporter), the government's balance sheet risk is reduced by ensuring that the strategic foreign currency benchmark is dominated by that currency.

A strategic benchmark for a debt manager can be regarded as replicating the asset side of a balance sheet. For a government debt manager, it represents the type of debt portfolio the government wishes to have, given the information available for assessing the risks on the asset side.

Because strategic benchmarks usually require the approval of the minister of finance or the executive branch of the government, they are a valuable guide for government debt managers in making their portfolio and risk management decisions.[2] For example, the risk management framework might include a requirement that all new funding and hedging transactions move the foreign currency portfolio closer to the strategic foreign currency benchmark portfolio. The characteristics of the benchmark portfolio will then guide the portfolio manager in making decisions on the final currency composition, interest rate sensitivity, and maturity of new borrowing, as well as on debt buyback operations and portfolio-hedging transactions.[3]

Framework for assessing portfolio performance

Portfolio benchmarks are also valuable for measuring portfolio performance in relation to cost, returns, and risk. Differences between the structure of the government's actual debt portfolio and its strategic debt portfolio as expressed by the benchmark indicate the degree to which government debt managers have succeeded in replicating the benchmark and thus moving the actual portfolio closer to the government's preferred composition. Interest rate risk, for example, can be measured by the extent to which the actual duration of the portfolio differs from the desired duration. Currency risk can be assessed by examining the difference between actual and desired currency composition. Portfolio benchmarks thus provide a means of measuring debt managers' performance and increasing their accountability.

Some governments (for example, those of Ireland, New Zealand, and Sweden) permit their debt managers to undertake tactical trading within specified position and loss limits. Position limits usually aggregate the amount of tactical exposure that is permissible and are typically expressed as acceptable deviations from a strategic benchmark. Tactical trading could be conducted in connection with the debt portfolio (for example, by using swaps and futures to move away from the duration target or to change the currency composition of the portfolio) or may involve discretion in investing the liquid asset portfolio. Value added is measured by whether, on a risk-adjusted basis, the tactical trading has generated positive returns. Some of the policy considerations in the use of tactical trading are discussed in chapter 5.

Usually, monitoring the actual portfolio in relation to the benchmarks and reporting on tactical trading are middle-office functions, given that portfolio managers should not be responsible for assessing their own performance. If the government's debt management is conducted outside the ministry of finance (e.g., by a separate debt agency or the central bank), the ministry of finance should retain some in-house expertise for developing benchmarks and analyzing performance.

Continuity in policy direction

By focusing debt managers' attention on the government's cost and risk objectives, strategic benchmarks can help foster maintenance of a risk management culture within the debt office and continuity of data gathering for risk analysis and reporting functions. This can be especially valuable when there is a high turnover of management and staff among government debt managers.

CHARACTERISTICS OF WELL-DESIGNED STRATEGIC BENCHMARKS

It is essential that the strategic benchmark be based on sound principles and analysis because benchmark risk is often one of the key risks that debt managers face. In many studies of asset-and-liability management performance, benchmark risk often accounts for in excess of 90 percent of total portfolio risk. Risk can be measured relative to the strategic benchmark, and in that sense replicating a benchmark could be considered a risk-neutral strategy. But all this depends critically on the integrity of the benchmark. If the strategic benchmark is poorly designed, it may itself represent an inferior portfolio configuration, and seeking to replicate it may result in poor cost and risk outcomes.

Although strategic benchmarks can be constructed using a variety of techniques and can be expressed in different ways, well-designed strategic benchmarks tend to share certain characteristics, as described next.

Incorporation of policy guidelines and macroeconomic objectives

Strategic benchmarks should reflect the government's debt management philosophy and its broad debt management goals. In addition, they should take into account important macroeconomic policy objectives. Doing so increases the potential for debt management policy and other macroeconomic policies to be mutually reinforcing and reduces the risk of policy tensions. For example, a government with a large fiscal deficit and a high ratio of net public sector debt to GDP may be anxious to reduce the volatility of its debt-servicing costs and may prefer to have a high proportion of fixed-rate rather than floating-rate debt in its portfolio. Alternatively, it may seek to lower debt servicing costs by financing at short maturities and taking the risk that the rolled-over debt is not more expensive. Similarly, when designing strategic foreign currency benchmarks, analysts should carefully examine the government's exchange rate objectives. If a country's currency is pegged to another currency or to a currency basket, the currency peg should be reflected in the design of the portfolio benchmark, since an alternative strategy (one that would involve borrowing in a different currency from the peg or in different proportions from the currency weights in the exchange rate basket) may begin to undermine the government's exchange rate policy and create policy tensions.

Incorporation of constraints

Strategic benchmarks should reflect the capital market constraints faced by the government and should be achievable, or replicable, over a reasonable time horizon. Countries with deep and liquid domestic markets for government fixed-income securities, such as France, Germany, Japan, and the United States, have a global investor base that absorbs their government financing needs, and they do not need to borrow in foreign currency. For many developing countries, however, the government's financing needs cannot be fully met through the domestic debt market, and foreign currency borrowing is required. In determining the maximum amount of their securities that the domestic debt market can absorb, governments must take into consideration the crowding-out effect that large amounts of government debt issuance may have, as well as the state of development of the domestic market. If that market is underdeveloped, the government may be compelled to issue short dated maturities. Strategic benchmarks should reflect such constraints and set targets that the government can realistically achieve.

Robustness

When constructing strategic benchmarks, the measures should be robust under a range of economic scenarios, time horizons, and analytical techniques.[4] If the benchmark is too dependent on the assumptions made or represents an efficient portfolio under one scenario only, it may have to be revised regularly, and the debt manager could be forced into frequent changes in direction. For example, the risk characteristics of a benchmark would differ depending on the assumptions about the shape of the yield curve and the way it might shift over time; the assumptions about economic growth and tax revenue that underpin the economic scenarios; the time period of the analysis; and whether extreme-case scenarios involving large and atypical interest rate movements are given material weight.[5] The objective should be to derive a strategic benchmark that is reasonably robust under a range of assumptions.

Care should be taken to ensure that the benchmarks are not simply an attempt to justify a current set of debt management strategies that may be suboptimal, and that they do not reflect personal views about future currency movements. Establishing benchmarks in such a way would be self-defeating. Nor should benchmarks be structured to be easily beatable, so that portfolio managers would be incorrectly perceived as adding a great deal of value in their borrowing and trading activities. Portfolio managers should not be permitted to set their own performance benchmarks. Instead, the risk analysis should be conducted by the risk management (or middle-office) specialists within the government debt management operation, working with staff from the ministry of finance.

IMPLEMENTING STRATEGIC BENCHMARKS

Once strategic benchmarks are in place, the government debt manager's role is to endeavor, over time, to move the risk characteristics of the actual portfolio closer to those embodied in the strategic benchmark portfolio.

How quickly this transformation can take place, and which instruments should be used, will depend on the nature of the constraints confronting the debt manager. If the debt manager does not have access to derivatives, the main vehicle for changing the composition of the government's foreign currency portfolio is likely to be the rolling off, or maturing, of loans and the initiation of new borrowing activities. Where the government has a strong presence in international capital markets, a sound sovereign credit rating, and access to financial derivatives, government debt managers may be able to employ currency swaps or buyback operations (using, for example, proceeds from privatizations) to transform the structure of the portfolio.

Decisions on new foreign currency borrowing should, whenever possible, be made with a view to reducing the differences in expected cost and risk between the actual portfolio and the benchmark portfolio. For example, if the actual portfolio relative to the benchmark portfolio is considered to be underweight in U.S. dollars and of shorter duration than desirable, the difference in risk between the two portfolios would be narrowed by a long-duration borrowing in U.S. dollars. Sometimes the debt managers may not be able to obtain the target duration in a particular currency. Provided that the government's foreign currency debt portfolio does not have excessive refinancing risk, the debt managers should endeavor to borrow in the desired currency (since currency risk is usually the dominant market risk in foreign currency portfolios) and attempt to refinance into longer maturities at a later stage. If the refinancing or rollover risk is already substantial, greater weight should be given to obtaining longer maturity borrowings. If the actual portfolio is aligned with the strategic benchmark, the government debt managers will need to make decisions on the degree to which they should rebalance the portfolio to counter duration drift.[6]

The elements making up the strategic benchmark, whether currency composition, interest rate duration, or target maturity, are typically expressed as ranges. Table 9 provides an illustration.

Table 9: Example of a foreign currency benchmark

	Foreign currency composition (percent)	Duration (years)
Currency 1	50 ± 5	3–4
Currency 2	25 ± 5	4–5
Currency 3	25 ± 5	2–3
Overall	**100**	**3–4**

If exchange rate and interest rate movements shift the composition of the actual portfolio outside the range of the strategic benchmark, the government debt manager will need to undertake transactions to bring the portfolio back within the benchmark. This can be done through currency swaps and new borrowing or, alternatively, by purchasing a foreign currency asset using domestic financing, provided that the duration objective is expressed in terms of net rather than gross foreign currency debt. Where derivatives such as swaps are used, the cost of taking on the additional credit exposure should be considered.[7]

Transactions to rebalance the portfolio result in transaction costs. Government debt managers generally prefer to have a reasonable range for the elements making up the benchmark in order to avoid incurring excessive transaction costs for what may be relatively small differences in risk. If the currency ranges in the benchmark target are too narrow, the government debt managers run the risk of being whipsawed—of having to make repeated trades to maintain the preferred exposure when faced with currency volatility. Narrow currency bands that require daily rebalancing of the government's debt portfolio to match a strategic benchmark are difficult to justify.

REVIEWING STRATEGIC BENCHMARKS

Since most of the market risk in asset-and-liability portfolios is associated with the selection of a strategic benchmark portfolio, rather than in any tactical trading around it, strategic benchmarks should be reviewed from time to time to assess their appropriateness. They should be revised if they have resulted in poor portfolio outcomes over a lengthy period, or the government's objectives change or there are significant shifts in economic relationships. Governments, for example, might reassess their risk tolerance following contagion experiences or banking crises. Alternatively, it might be necessary to modify benchmarks in the light of large mineral or energy discoveries, the introduction of a new currency such as the euro, a policy decision by the government to eliminate its net foreign currency debt, or a sustained period of structural adjustment reform that makes historical relationships between domestic and foreign interest rates and exchange rate relationships less relevant as a basis for formulating a portfolio management strategy.[8]

Strategic benchmarks should not be changed simply because colleagues within the debt office have particular views about future interest rates or exchange rates. Nor should they be modified because relative prices such as the exchange rate move in an unanticipated manner over a short period of time, unless there is evidence of an expected permanent shift in market relationships due to changing structural forces. Any recommendation to change the strategic benchmark should be discussed with the minister of finance.

ESTABLISHING STRATEGIC BENCHMARKS AT EARLY STAGES IN THE DEVELOPMENT OF GOVERNMENT DEBT MANAGEMENT

Unlike many OECD countries, developing countries often have to borrow in foreign currency to meet domestic financing gaps (the shortfall in domestic savings relative to investment needs), to reduce their refinancing risk by lengthening the maturity of their borrowing, or to finance reserves.[9] Some governments also believe that it is important to establish a foreign currency pricing benchmark to help the private sector develop a borrowing presence in foreign currency markets.

Between October 1997 and November 1999, the number of IBRD borrowing countries that had introduced strategic benchmarks as part of their government debt management increased from 2 to 10. Many of these countries were also endeavoring to establish a middle office. Countries with strategic benchmarks tended to set specific targets for the currency mix, for the share of fixed-rate versus floating-rate debt, and sometimes for the share of foreign currency debt versus local currency debt. Most also specified the preferred amortization and maturity profile of the debt. Another 10 countries, although not using strategic benchmarks, had established guidelines for managing the government's debt. These guidelines usually sought to address refinancing risk and also specified the types of currencies that the government could borrow in.

Most of the 20 countries that said they used benchmarks or risk guidelines were also using a variety of techniques for analyzing the cost and risk of the debt. The types of risk analysis being conducted included debt sustainability analysis, scenario analysis, and value-at-risk or cost-at-risk measures to test the sensitivity of the cost of debt. Although the number of countries using these risk analysis tools has grown since 1997, most IBRD borrowing countries still indicated that their governments were not undertaking risk analysis of government debt.

Introducing an initial strategic benchmark need not require detailed or sophisticated risk analysis. Governments that are less advanced in their risk analysis but that have large foreign currency debt portfolios and access to a number of currencies can adopt measures to substantially reduce their currency risk. Useful guidelines for portfolio managers can be developed by considering a number of fundamental economic factors. For example, in designing an initial benchmark, valuable insights can be gained by examining the exchange rate regime and the degree of integration (through trade, capital flows, and other financial flows) between the home country and its trading partners. If, for example, the currency is pegged under a credible exchange rate regime, the currency forming the peg is likely to dominate the choice of currency in the strategic benchmark.

If the country has a floating exchange rate, the design of the strategic benchmark could be based on considerations relating to the currencies that dominate the country's trade and capital flows; on historical analysis of which currencies have been least volatile relative to the domestic currency or have been cheaper (even though the expected cost of borrowing in foreign currencies is the same); or on the size of major economies or groups of economies relative to indicators such as global market output or world bond market capitalization. The last approach can be particularly important when a government has little idea as to what its strategic benchmark should be. Then, currency diversification may be a particularly appropriate strategy. The rationale for this strategy is based on considerations similar to those faced by an asset manager who endeavors to diversify risk efficiently by "buying the market." In adopting a diversification, or "sell the market," strategy, the debt manager could use GDP weights or bond market capitalization to determine the structure of the strategic benchmark. The currency composition of the benchmark might be based on the relative share in world output or world bond market capitalization of the United States, the euro zone countries, and Japan. A duration target in each major currency could be based on the duration of the government bond market in the country concerned or on the weighted average of the treasury bill and government bond market. This choice could be justified on the grounds that the duration established by one of the major developed countries for its domestic currency government debt issuance is likely to reflect an efficient cost and risk tradeoff for the issuer. A band could be established around the target to form a duration range.

These risk management issues are especially difficult for developing country governments that are dependent on multilateral borrowing and donor funding. Some multilateral agencies offer borrowers a choice of currency, but this option is not available to the low-income countries that borrow from the World Bank's International Development Association (IDA); instead, donor funding is usually denominated in the donors' currencies. Where IDA countries do not have access to currency choice, they can end up with currency exposures that pose substantial risk for them. There is little that these countries can do to change the exposures other than to discuss the issue with donor governments.

These are only indicative examples of a possible approach; many sensible alternative structures exist. But the main point should not be lost. Even governments that lack sophisticated risk analysis tools and years of continuous data series on interest rates and exchange rates can still do a great deal to reduce the riskiness of their debt portfolios and balance sheets by exploring from first principles the economic characteristics that could guide the design of an initial strategic benchmark. The results of such a fundamental examination may be of great assistance in reducing the riskiness of government debt portfolios.

NOTES

1. As discussed in chapter 4, in the absence of this matching, the government's overall balance sheet risk increases as the debt office and central bank take on different currency and interest rate exposures.

2. In Denmark the currency allocation for the central government's net foreign currency assets (reserves minus foreign currency debt) is approved by the minister of finance, and the Nationalbanken is responsible for managing the foreign currency debt. In Belgium and Colombia, the minister of finance and the government debt managers hold regular discussions on the structure of the liability benchmark portfolio.

3. Borrowing could be in a different currency or duration, but the government would then need to swap into its preferred currency and duration. Borrowing and swapping may prove to be a cheaper way of obtaining the desired currency exposure than borrowing in the final currency directly.

4. A variety of analytical methods should be used in managing the government's risk. For example, a portfolio characterized by a barbell structure and another represented by discount bonds with the same overall duration can represent very different portfolio risks. Duration targets alone often indicate very little about the maturity structure of the debt, and the government may be exposed to substantially different refinancing risks under the two structures. This highlights the need for combining duration analysis with other risk analysis.

5. Government debt managers have to worry about extreme outcomes—even those that are considered to have a low probability—because extreme market movements in interest and exchange rates can lead to default. It is important to stress-test the cash flow scenarios for these low-probability, high-risk outcomes.

6. *Duration drift* refers to the decline in the duration or interest rate sensitivity of a bond as the time to maturity decreases, all other things being unchanged.

7. Pricing credit risk can be complicated, and few government debt managers have introduced credit-pricing models. Many government debt managers have, however, developed credit-pricing rules whereby lower funding costs or, in the case of investment portfolios, higher returns (measured in basis points) are required in order to compensate the debt manager for the additional credit risk involved.

8. Following the introduction of the euro in 1999, a number of European government debt management offices that had previously borrowed in European currencies replaced their foreign currency benchmarks with a domestic currency benchmark based on the euro. In many of these countries the main emphasis in government debt management is on reducing expected debt-servicing costs or domestic interest rate risk.

9. In Canada, New Zealand, and the United Kingdom, government foreign currency borrowing is only undertaken to finance foreign currency reserves. In these cases the currency and interest rate characteristics of the government's foreign currency borrowing are guided by the risk characteristics of the foreign currency reserves, and the government's foreign currency debt is fully or largely immunized.

Chapter 8

Investing in Management Information Systems

In the early 1990s, many of what are today considered leading government debt management offices were recording transactions in handwritten ledgers or on whiteboards. Their portfolios were not marked-to-market, calculation of portfolio duration was difficult, only rudimentary scenario analysis was possible, and measures such as cost at risk were still a decade away from common use. Since then, the complexity of the decisions and transactions handled by government debt managers has increased greatly, and the tools available for dealing with debt management have been transformed. A key question facing many governments in developing countries is whether to adopt computerized systems and, if so, how sophisticated and comprehensive those systems need to be.

Sound management information systems are essential for asset and liability management, but their development poses major challenges—for government debt managers and corporate treasurers alike. Systems development is an area in which large amounts of money and of management and staff time can be deployed and expensive mistakes can easily be made. Government debt managers invariably spend a great deal of time on systems-related management issues.

This chapter discusses the core information systems functionality that government debt managers require, the issues involved in managing systems investments, and the management information needed to manage a government debt portfolio. These considerations also apply to other government institutions with responsibility for managing asset or liability portfolios, such as central banks in their management of foreign currency reserves.

CORE FUNCTIONALITY REQUIREMENTS

Although the sophistication of the information systems needed by government debt offices differs depending on the risk characteristics of the portfolio being managed, all government debt managers require accurate and reliable management information systems and, just as important, need to understand how the systems data are derived and how to interpret the output.

For government debt managers who manage large and risky government debt portfolios that include foreign currency transactions, the following core functionality is usually required:

- *Capture of market data.* If government debt managers are undertaking public issues, conducting hedging and buyback transactions, or trading tactically with a view to making risk-adjusted returns, they will need access to live prices, such as spot and forward exchange and interest rates, swap market spreads, and secondary market spreads. If a significant part of the portfolio is being actively traded (say, because of a decision to trade a liquidity portfolio tactically), or if hedges such as swaps have collateral requirements attached to them based on the market value of the hedge, it will be necessary to mark to market those components of the portfolio.

- *Risk and performance analysis.* This could include such elements as scenario analysis for assessing cost-risk tradeoffs; information on budget at risk or cost at risk; comparisons between the composition of the actual portfolio and of the benchmark portfolio; tactical trading performance relative to position limits and loss limits; and an assessment of credit exposure against counterparty credit limits.

- *Debt recording and debt analysis.* A general ledger capability is needed to account for transactions and to record debt-servicing obligations. Information on the debt profile, such as principal amortization schedules, amount of debt outstanding, and due dates for debt-servicing payments, is necessary for managing liquidity, preventing default, and assisting with reporting needs (budget tables, reports to the sovereign credit rating agencies, and the like).

It may not be possible to capture all these capabilities in one system. If additional systems are involved, it is important that they share a common database or data warehouse to satisfy concerns about data integrity and security.

Starting up a computerized system

The introduction of a computerized debt management information system is only likely to succeed if a well-maintained manual debt-recording system is already in place and is being supported by sound legal and administrative arrangements and accurate loan data. If the quality of government debt management is being impeded by legal ambiguity, unclear roles, an inadequate control environment, and poor practices in administrative design and in the overall management of information exchange, computerizing the loan book is unlikely to add any value. It is difficult to overstate the importance of dealing with such issues before introducing a computerized debt-recording system, or the importance of cleaning the existing loan data and replacing missing data. It may take several months to recover missing loan data (recourse often being made to the lender for documentation) and to clean, or undertake due diligence on, the data already contained in the manual system.

Assuming that these prerequisite conditions have been met, the key element needed by countries just starting out is a debt management system that can record the government's debt cash flows on both an individual transaction and a consolidated portfolio basis. Centralizing the database is critical so that the government can readily determine its overall indebtedness, reduce the risk of defaulting on obligations because of poor-quality data or poor management procedures, and begin to assess its portfolio risk. The minimum functionalities required are the ability to capture the cash flow details of all borrowing transactions—including currency denomination, interest rate basis, any option characteristics, debt-servicing and principal repayment amounts, payment dates, and the names of counterparties—and a capability for processing settlements.

In most countries, the central bank is the government's banker, and all government payments and receipts flow through the government's account at the central bank. If the central bank is the paying agent for the government debt managers, the bank will require complete information on payment obligations and will need to have an agreement with the debt managers on payment instructions and procedures. The government debt managers will have to monitor the government's bank account balances regularly.

In the early stages, front-office technology with market data feeds is only important when the government is undertaking borrowing and hedging transactions directly in the market. If the government's financing gap is met through donor grants, official aid flows, or IDA credits, government debt managers are unlikely to need access to market feeds.

Increasingly, however, government debt managers in developing countries have to be familiar with market-based financial products. Many multilateral development banks now offer lending products that are priced off market indices and contain embedded options that can be exercised at the discretion of the borrower. Some of these development banks also give borrowers access to freestanding hedges (such as currency and interest rate swaps, and interest rate caps and collars) that can be used to transform the risk exposure on existing government debt owed to the institution.[1]

Risk analysis features become important when the portfolio is large and complex. Basic risk analysis can be spreadsheet based because the objective of the initial analysis is to obtain an understanding of the orders of magnitude of the risks over a long time horizon. It is only when more sophisticated risk analysis of the portfolio is needed (for example, when portfolios are actively traded and risk is managed on a real-time basis) that specific risk management software may be required.

Many World Bank borrowers have introduced either the UNCTAD or the Commonwealth Secretariat (COMSEC) debt-recording system into their debt management operations.[2] These systems enable governments to record and monitor their external debt and their government-guaranteed debt and on-lending, make debt-servicing projections, and perform sensitivity analysis vis-à-vis exchange rate and interest rate movements. The systems' interface with the World Bank Debt Strategy Module allows debt managers to carry out macroeconomic and balance of payments analysis.

Characteristics of good debt management systems

Good debt management systems should have broad functionality that enables debt managers to record cash flows accurately for all transactions they undertake and to translate these flows into present values when necessary. The cash flows involved are those associated with foreign currency and domestic currency borrowings, hedging and trading activities, guarantees, and on-lending. Given the option-like characteristics of guarantees, their valuation requires the estimation of expected cost, which may have to be done using separate software.

It is desirable that debt management systems draw on a single source or a limited number of sources for all core data and that the data module cover all or a substantial part of the flow of transactions from the front to the back office. Linkages to market information services such as Reuters, Telerate, and Bloomberg and to electronic banking and payment services such as SWIFT should be available. Whenever feasible, manual processing of data should be minimized. The systems should be able to ensure the integrity of the data produced and permit further development and interfacing. All data and applications should be portable and open so that several users can simultaneously have access to real-time data. The systems should be user friendly and easy to maintain and should be accompanied by good user documentation and security features.

Relatively few integrated treasury systems now on the market have fully developed functionality for front-, middle-, and back-office operations. Often, the front-office (and sometimes the back-office) applications are well developed while the middle-office functions are confined to a small number of pricing and performance analogs, such as value at risk, that may not be suitable for the debt managers' needs. The middle-office risk analysis, performance measurement, and monitoring functionality may have to be extensively customized, which can be expensive and time consuming, or additional specialized middle-office systems that are compatible with the original system may have to be acquired.

Except for the UNCTAD and COMSEC systems, most of the off-the-shelf management information systems used by government debt managers are designed for banks, other financial intermediaries, or large corporate treasuries that may actively trade their portfolios. Such systems are designed primarily for managing foreign currency portfolios rather than domestic debt portfolios, and they may not work well for domestic cash management. In addition, many domestic currency borrowing instruments, such as retail bonds and inflation-adjusted bonds, have unique characteristics, and the debt management system may not be able to record automatically all aspects of cash flow. In that case, debt managers need to decide whether to standardize and simplify the domestic debt instruments currently in use or to maintain them in their existing form and record them in a different debt-recording system—which can mean developing another database.

The features of the management information system, and the debt managers' understanding of them, should set limits on the range of debt management transactions. The system should provide complete coverage of all the financial instruments that the government debt manager uses. Where it does not, and the cash flows of a particular instrument cannot be readily captured in a separate system, that instrument should not be used. Debt managers are on dangerous ground when they enter into trades that cannot be accurately captured by their debt-recording systems or are not fully understood by the portfolio managers and risk managers. When the debt managers understand all aspects of the transaction but the debt-recording system is unable to record the trade or monitor payment flows (e.g., when these flows depend on specific market prices such as the price of a particular commodity or index of commodities), such transactions should not be undertaken except under special circumstances and unless the cash flows can be easily recorded and monitored on a separate spreadsheet or other software.

Management information reporting needs

Reporting needs for the management information system will depend on the nature of the portfolio and the government's debt management goals. Assuming that a sound debt management framework is in place, the following information is required for managing a sizeable foreign currency and domestic currency debt portfolio:

- The debt-servicing and principal payments due on every loan, expressed in the relevant currency.

- The aggregate repayments of principal and debt-servicing costs due in each currency each year.

- The proportions of fixed-rate and floating-rate debt, disaggregated by currency and year.

- The cash flow details of all the loans that are callable by the government.

- The cash flow details of all swap-driven transactions, including the name of the counterparty to the swap, the market value of the swap and its interest rate sensitivity, the call dates on the swap, and the market value of any collateral that has been paid or received on the swap.

- The marked-to-market valuation of calls on outstanding borrowings, and the market value of calls on swaps.

- The aggregate market exposure (swaps, on-lending, and investment positions associated with the management of a liquidity portfolio) of each counterparty in relation to the aggregate credit exposure permissible under the debt office's credit policy.[3]

- The amount of liquidity on hand compared with the levels of liquidity prescribed under the liquidity policy.

- The market value of tactical trading positions and the profit and loss generated on these activities compared with established position and loss limits.

- Comparison of the risk characteristics of the government's debt portfolio with the ranges set for the government's strategic benchmarks. This would probably include targets for duration, currency composition, and maturities. It may also involve comparison of actual cash flows with the cash flow simulations used in scenario analysis.

It is only necessary to mark the portfolio to market when the debt office is involved in activities such as exercise of calls in the portfolio, debt buyback operations, and tactical trading or where payment obligations vary according to changes in market prices (for example, payment obligations under swaps or other forward transactions). If these types of activity are not undertaken, the government is a passive portfolio manager, and it is not necessary to have the portfolio marked to market unless particular accounting conventions call for it.[4]

Information for monitoring the efficiency of cash management by government-funded agencies and government departments is also needed: an example might be comparison of the actual cash balances of individual government departments with those forecast by departments (and vetted by the finance ministry) on daily, weekly, and monthly bases. This information is often collected by the ministry of finance (rather than the debt managers) as part of its financial management controls across government agencies. Aside from helping to ensure that government agencies are managing their cash needs efficiently, the information is needed by the debt managers for determining the size of daily open-market operations to offset the liquidity flows between the government and the banking system.

When the debt office trades its own debt in the domestic market, the management information needs for a portfolio of only domestic currency debt are similar to those for a combined domestic and foreign currency debt portfolio. If government debt managers do not engage in debt trading (and very few do) and do not issue callable bonds, the core information needed for the domestic debt portfolio is limited to principal and debt-servicing obligations, refinancing risk, and repricing risk (the mix of fixed-rate and floating-rate debt). Some debt managers have also developed budget-at-risk and cost-at-risk measures for the domestic currency debt portfolio and use these measures to guide their issuance strategies.

Developing and implementing a systems strategy

Regardless of whether government debt managers intend to build their own systems, contract from a third party, or purchase and customize an off-the-shelf system (as discussed in the next section), a number of conditions have to be satisfied if the systems are to meet user needs on time and within budget. Among the most important steps in developing a systems strategy are to:

- Define the objectives of the systems project carefully in both general and specific terms, ensure their consistency with broader business development plans, and obtain the strong support of senior management for the investment.

- Establish a strong project management team whose decisionmaking is governed by sound management processes.

- Document the existing system's output and the transaction steps and data flows associated with the debt management operation.

- Undertake a comprehensive business process reengineering review to examine how existing business processes, systems, and information flows, including transaction flows, can be improved. All staff should be involved in this process, but the role of the business analysts on the project team is particularly important. These analysts' job is to understand the organization's business objectives and the requirements of individual users and to communicate these objectives and needs effectively to the information technology specialists.

- Work with users to develop an accurate definition of user requirements and to determine how sophisticated the overall system and its key features need to be—whether, for example, users require integrated databases and applications, portability of applications, or openness to development and interfacing. It is important to distinguish essential functionality from features that are desirable but not critical.

- Write detailed user specifications.

- Determine whether the functionality should be developed in-house or purchased from a systems provider—in the latter case, by leasing or otherwise contracting technology services from an outside provider or by buying an off-the-shelf system that will be customized in-house or by outside contractors.

- If a system is to be acquired from outside, establish short-listing criteria and appropriate procedures for searching for and procuring a system. The latter include procedures for issuing requests for information and requests for proposals, evaluating proposals, testing short-listed systems applications, and checking reference sites and the experiences of other users.

The importance of establishing a strong systems project management capability cannot be overemphasized. Appointment of an experienced project manager is essential, as is clarity concerning the roles of senior management and the project steering committee in project management. Sound management procedures relating to the preparation and monitoring of budgets, timetables, and deliverables are needed, along with a clear understanding of reporting requirements, performance incentives and sanctions, and the value that comments by outside peer reviewers can add to the quality of project implementation.

Systems projects are, in essence, change management projects. They require all the careful planning and management needed for a major enterprise restructuring or rationalization, where success depends on the quality of the strategy and on its implementation. The latter is critically dependent on the extent to which staff in the debt office accept the need for change and feel empowered to carry it out. Development of a sound project management capability requires strong leadership—not simply support from the project sponsor, who is usually the head of the debt management office.

Failed management information systems projects exact a high cost in money, lost opportunities, and low morale. When systems projects are unsuccessful, it is often because of lack of leadership and a clear commitment by senior management. Systems staff, including the project management team, perceive that senior management is not fully behind the systems investment and is unwilling to provide the budget and resources to support it.

Systems projects may also fail because project managers are not able to convince users of the need for systems change and secure their support and ownership responsibility for the project. This situation often arises when the deficiencies of the present systems are not widely understood and the overall goals, user requirements, and specifications of the systems change are not identified clearly and early enough. The problems are accentuated if a viable project strategy is not prepared and adhered to and if budgeting, priority-setting, monitoring, and reporting procedures are inadequate. The project dies because staff members are not convinced of the need for change and lack confidence in the ability of the project management team to deliver what it has promised.

Still another reason for failure is the selection of a system that requires excessive customization at an early stage or that is ill suited to debt managers' needs. The functionality of debt-recording systems and risk management systems is often very sophisticated and may not be readily understood by all members of the project steering committee. Before requesting proposals from systems providers, it is essential to take the time to clarify user requirements, assess whether they are realistic, and determine which features are indispensable.

Criteria for short-listing the responses to the requests for proposal are usually based on gap analysis comparing the functionality contained in the system with that desired. The criteria should include considerations such as price (although this is usually negotiable and large discounts are often possible), vendor reputation, software support, the estimated cost of the customization required, and comments by users in similar businesses. It may also be prudent to review the vendor's financial background.

Once a short list of systems providers has been prepared, all features of the preferred systems should be thoroughly tested, using sample transaction data. Users should be heavily involved in short-listing systems, testing them, and making the final selection. This process is essential in order to gauge the quality of the system's fit, garner support for the project among a wide range of users, and gather information on the type of customization needed.

Even when an appropriate system is selected, systems projects are often less than fully successful because inadequate measures are taken in the early stages to review and improve business processes and to address data deficiencies. Some of the principal gains from systems projects come from reviewing the business strategy in the light of the expected enhancements to productivity resulting from the systems investment. These important benefits can be lost if steps are not taken to appraise the integration of the systems strategy with the business strategy and to examine whether business processes can be reengineered to enhance efficiency.

BUSINESS CONTINUITY PLANNING

It is important to develop comprehensive business recovery procedures to ensure that government debt management operations can continue to operate in the event of natural disasters or other events. The debt office should identify the types of disaster scenario it wishes to protect against and assess the associated risks to financial, physical, and human capital. Procedures should be developed for storing backup tapes and for coping with temporary work stoppages, perhaps through arrangements for working at home or from a nearby building. To protect against more serious and prolonged disaster scenarios, consideration should be given to establishing "cold," "warm," or "hot" sites as business backup facilities. (The terms refer to the amount of preparation required to enable operations to resume in another location—often, in another city—in the event of a major natural disaster or communications failure.) At a minimum it is essential to ensure access to the systems data and networks required to manage the portfolios and to identify in advance the critical functions that need to be undertaken in a business continuity setting.

Options for acquiring systems: in-house, third-party provider, or customization

Governments wishing to improve the quality of their debt management invariably face systems challenges. For example, government debt managers may be operating legacy systems that were originally developed for budget-recording purposes within the ministry of finance at a time when the debt portfolio was small and contained little risk. Such systems may be ill suited for managing large, complex debt portfolios and may require considerable manual intervention and external servicing to operate and maintain. Given these problems and the lack of integration with other in-house systems, debt managers often need to invest in a replacement system.

Government debt managers have the choice of buying an off-the-shelf system, purchasing information technology services from an external provider, or building a system in-house. There is no definitive right way; examples can be found of debt offices that have used any one of these methods or have developed a mixture of off-the-shelf and in-house systems.[5]

A major benefit of building a management information system in-house is that the project, if successful, is more likely than an off-the-shelf system to meet the special needs of government debt managers. The unique features required can be built in and modified as needed. But there are important cost and risk considerations. Building a sophisticated in-house system takes considerable expertise and a large investment in staff and management time over several years, and it diverts resources from other projects and priorities. In-house systems often do not get completed because of the types of management failures referred to in the previous section. In addition, in-house development of new applications can create "key person" risk, in that debt managers can become dependent on in-house systems expertise for undertaking systems development—although high-quality systems documentation can mitigate the problem. There is also a substantial risk that the in-house developers will not be able to replicate the enhancements that vendors provide in their new releases and upgrades. If the debt managers want these features, they will have to purchase additional software and develop separate infrastructure to support it. In-house systems can be expensive to maintain if they are developed on hardware platforms that become obsolete and that systems vendors decline to support, choosing instead to focus on more recent products.

Contracting information technology services from a third party can generate substantial savings over time in the form of reduced development and maintenance costs, and it allows for access to systems upgrades and enhancements. This type of contracting is feasible for standard debt management functions such as capturing market data, pricing transactions, and settling trades. But some of the debt managers' needs can only be met by customizing systems applications (e.g., for cash management purposes or for borrowing through nonstandard instruments), and these enhancements may not be available through outsourcing.

With an off-the-shelf system, the debt managers do not have to build the basic core system, and they retain access to future upgrades. Debt managers will have to decide whether to acquire a single fully integrated system or integrated compartmentalized systems. They also need to decide whether to purchase rights to access the data model and so enable in-house customization, or whether to run the risk of being dependent on the systems vendor or other outside contractors for adapting code to meet user needs.

But purchase of an off-the-shelf system has its disadvantages. Many such systems were designed primarily as asset management tools and require considerable customization if acquired for government debt management purposes. In that case, the debt managers may essentially be developing an in-house system. The need for customization is usually greatest for front-office cash management, middle-office risk management, and back-office general ledger operations. In the front office, the off-the-shelf applications may not cover debt instruments that are specific to the local market, and a special cash management module may have to be created. In the middle office, the systems modules may contain standard products such as value-at-risk analogs, but these may not be very helpful if little tactical trading is undertaken and the office has developed its own risk measures to monitor and review portfolio positions. The general ledger needs of the back office will depend on the nature of the instruments traded and the range of counterparties involved in transactions. Considerable care is needed to ensure that the accounting ledger is compatible with national accounting standards.

Debt managers can become very dependent on the systems supplier for developing enhancements, upgrades, and workarounds and for debugging faulty software. If the system is customized by outside providers, this, too, can become a source of dependency. Managing the relationship with the vendor or service provider can consume substantial management time, particularly if the systems provider's software development program and the content of new software releases are focused on private sector clients with large budgets (e.g., asset managers and commercial banks) rather than on government debt management clients. After-sales support, access to new product enhancements, and terms for customization should all be part of the purchase contract.

Irrespective of whether the information systems are purchased, built in-house, or contracted from an external provider, debt managers need to specify their requirements carefully and invest in the types of capacity building illustrated in chapter 10. Doing so helps clarify expectations among systems users and avoids the situation, which is unfortunately too frequently encountered, where the debt manager and systems provider are unsure about what they are trying to build. This can be a particular concern for risk modeling systems, as users can have unrealistic expectations of acquiring a system and having a large array of relevant risk modeling reporting immediately available.

NOTES

1. Lending products of the European Bank for Reconstruction and Development (EBRD), the International Finance Corporation (IFC), and the World Bank are priced off the London interbank offered rate (LIBOR) or a comparable market index and contain embedded hedges to help clients manage their financial risks. The World Bank has also introduced

freestanding hedges for borrowers that enable them to restructure the risk characteristics of their existing IBRD loans.

2. UNCTAD's debt management software is the Debt Management and Financial Analysis System (DMFAS). The COMSEC system is the Commonwealth Secretariat Debt Recording and Management System (CS-DRMS). See the further discussion in chapter 10.

3. The debt managers may also require the capacity to net some exposures, where this is considered legally robust.

4. In this situation the government's debt management strategy would bear some similarity to that of a buy-and-hold investor. The government would simply hold its liabilities until they matured.

5. For example, Ireland's National Treasury Management Agency has successfully built its own debt-recording systems but also uses middle-office software, acquired from a systems vendor, for assessing risk management strategies. The New Zealand Debt Management Office has replaced its in-house systems with a customized off-the-shelf integrated front-, middle-, and back-office system; the Swedish National Debt Office has a combination of off-the-shelf and in-house management information systems.

Chapter 9

The Importance of Developing Domestic Government Bond Markets

Efficient government bond and money markets can yield substantial benefits, and most governments seek to play a catalytic role in fostering their growth. The markets in question include the interbank market, the short-term money market (for treasury bills and repo governments, among others), and the government fixed-income market. For most governments, the development and maintenance of these markets should be an essential element of balance sheet management.

Two situations arise in which exceptions to this important policy goal might be warranted. The first is in small economies, where the costs of establishing and supporting the necessary market infrastructure, including an adequate regulatory and supervisory framework, and of providing sufficient liquidity may be large in relation to the potential transaction base.[1] The second is the case in which a government has had several years of fiscal surpluses, which are expected to continue. The government then may have the option of paying off its gross debt, rather than establishing a large asset portfolio and maintaining a government bond market.[2]

Leaving aside these special cases, this chapter examines why governments should want to encourage well-performing government bond markets and summarizes some of the issues involved in helping to create them.[3]

THE BENEFITS OF AN EFFICIENT BOND MARKET

An efficient, or deep and liquid, government bond market is characterized by low transaction costs, competitive market processes, a sound market infrastructure, a large investor base, and high substitutability between financial instruments. In such markets, a diverse range of transactors can execute large trades quickly, producing only limited movements in price, and the market generally demonstrates considerable resilience in responding to financial and economic disturbances. (For further elaboration, see BIS 1999.)

Above all, government securities markets increase the efficiency and completeness of the domestic capital market. Generation of market interest rates that reflect the true opportunity cost of financing across a range of maturities facilitates the allocation of capital to productive uses. Financing and investment decisions can be taken that reflect the true cost of capital to the institution concerned.[4] Both the government and the private sector gain.

Benefits for the government

More options for fiscal adjustment and government financing. Government bond markets assist governments in their macroeconomic management by giving them additional freedom in responding to budgetary shocks. Rather than sharply adjusting spending and tax rates, governments are able to spread or smooth fiscal adjustment over a longer period.[5] Government bond markets also provide the means for a government to finance its spending in a noninflationary manner by borrowing from the private sector rather than from the central bank. Borrowing from the central bank does allow the government to finance its spending in domestic currency (for a time, at least) and enables the central bank to generate seigniorage. But the high rates of inflation that such borrowing can generate can significantly and adversely affect actual and potential economic growth by distorting relative price signals, eroding competitiveness, and undermining incentives to save and to invest in productive assets.[6]

Access to diverse sources of funding and liberation from captive lending arrangements. Where liquid and efficient bond markets exist, the government does not have to rely on captive domestic banks and other intermediaries for budgetary financing. Dependence on captive funding sources can have several negative effects. It distorts the portfolio allocation decisions of these intermediaries and constrains their ability to lend to the private sector. It also reduces the intermediaries' income, since governments in many countries pay below-market interest rates for this forced lending. Furthermore, these borrowing arrangements can create contingent liabilities for the government in the event of systemic failure within the domestic banking system. This occurred in Korea in the late 1990s, when the Korean government's dependence on domestic banks for budgetary financing added to the pressures it faced to guarantee the banks' foreign currency loans.

Independent operation of monetary policy and debt management policy. As discussed in chapter 2, well-developed money and bond markets permit the independent operation of monetary policy and debt management policy. Government debt managers are able to issue securities directly in the primary market, while the central bank can alter monetary conditions by buying and selling securities in the secondary market.

To sum up, a diversified and efficient domestic financial market gives the government a greater choice of funding sources and provides readily accessible funding, helping to buffer the effects of domestic and international financial shocks on the real economy.[7] This broader access to funding can be especially valuable in times of global financial instability, when countries— in particular, those with below–investment grade credit ratings—may experience difficulty in obtaining foreign currency financing. In the absence of a well-developed domestic bond market, a sharp curtailment of voluntary international lending to these countries can increase the risks of default on the government's foreign currency obligations and of large output and employment losses. When the revenue streams available to the government for servicing its debt are denominated in domestic currency and are not very sensitive to exchange rate movements, borrowing in domestic currency can help the government reduce its overall balance sheet risk.

Private sector benefits

Government bond markets generate important externalities for the private sector as well, particularly in situations where incomplete credit markets reflect an unwillingness of private sector transactors to enter into long-term financial contracts.

Greater predictability and increased competition. A government's benchmark yield curve is a valuable reference for pricing public and private sector financial contracts (e.g., bonds issued by state-owned enterprises and private sector corporations) and can help lessen price uncertainty, reduce transaction costs, and support the development of longer-term contractual arrangements throughout the economy. Over time, the development of corporate bond markets reduces corporations' dependence on commercial banks and increases competitive pressures on banks and other lending institutions to reduce their lending margins and develop more innovative products.

Development of hedges. Liquid government bond markets facilitate the development of a range of fixed-income derivatives products—such as swaps, repurchase agreements, futures, and options—that can be used to hedge financial risk on individual transactions or at the portfolio level. These hedging contracts are contingent claims whose price depends on that of the underlying bond market instrument. They in turn contribute to the creation of additional liquidity in the domestic bond market, as the underlying bonds can be used, along with derivatives, to help structure suitable hedges.

A government bond is usually the highest-rated domestic financial instrument in the economy and is often considered to be a credit risk–free asset when the government has a AAA credit rating in its domestic currency. Since credit risk premia increase with time to maturity, long-dated AAA-rated government securities are valuable for meeting the balance sheet hedging needs of investors with long-term liabilities denominated in domestic currency, especially when these obligations are indexed to the price level and inflation-indexed government bonds are available as hedges. Several governments, in an attempt to encourage and mobilize household savings, have marketed government bonds at the retail level; some of these are inflation indexed. Retail instruments have played an important role in government debt management in Canada, France, Germany, Ireland, Portugal, Sweden, and the United Kingdom.[8]

CHOICES IN THE DEVELOPMENT OF A GOVERNMENT BOND MARKET

The considerations discussed above illustrate the importance of making the development of a viable domestic money market and fixed-income market a key part of the government's debt management strategy and its broader balance sheet management. They help explain why the government of Singapore, for example, embarked on a bond issuance strategy in May 2000 that was aimed at making available large volumes of liquid domestic government bonds, even though the economy's domestic savings rate is high and the government has a strong balance sheet and a reputation for prudent fiscal management.

One of the important decisions a government faces is whether to concentrate its issuance on nominal or price-indexed bonds, as discussed next.

Price-indexed versus nominal bonds

Governments often issue nominal and price-indexed bonds side by side. Doing so can help broaden a government's funding sources and assist investors in diversifying their investment portfolios. Comparison of the yields on nominal and price-indexed bonds can provide the government and the market with valuable information on inflationary expectations.

Nominal fixed-income securities are the dominant bond instrument in most domestic bond markets.[9] With these instruments, the investor, rather than the government, bears the risk of higher-than-expected inflation, even though the market's view of expected inflation will be reflected in the price the investor pays for the bonds. A government issuing nominal bonds is exposed to the risk that inflation may turn out to be much lower than was expected when the bonds were issued and priced, which would increase the real debt-servicing burden.

Nominal fixed-rate instruments can be valuable to the issuer in extending portfolio duration. As discussed in chapter 4, they can be particularly useful for helping to hedge a government's fiscal position or balance sheet risk against supply shocks. For example, should an adverse supply-side shock or terms of trade shock increase domestic prices, causing output to decline and the government's budgetary position to deteriorate, nominal bonds would help stabilize debt-servicing costs and offset the deterioration in the government's fiscal accounts. Indexed debt would increase debt-servicing costs at a time when the government's tax revenue had declined.

Price-indexed debt, by contrast, provides a good hedge against the effects of temporary negative demand shocks. To illustrate, a rise in the household savings ratio or an adverse financial shock would be expected, in the short term, to result in a decline in output and inflation and a deterioration in the government's fiscal position. Debt-servicing costs would be lower for price-indexed debt than for nominal bonds and would help hedge the government's fiscal position.[10]

When real, or price-indexed, bonds are issued, the government, rather than the investor, bears the risk of inflation—although the risk to the government's balance sheet is reduced to the extent that the cash flows available for servicing the debt are also indexed, as is usually the case for tax revenues. Because the government assumes the inflation risk, it can often set longer maturities for price-indexed bonds. These bonds can be a valuable investment vehicle for institutions such as pension funds, which may have long-term expenditure obligations indexed to inflation, or for other investors worried about the risk of inflation.

The effects of issuance of these different types of bond on the government's debt-servicing costs depend on whether the time path of inflation turns out to be lower than investors originally allowed for in pricing nominal bonds. Investors will be willing to accept lower real returns on price-indexed bonds than they expect on nominal bonds, provided that the premium they pay for inflation certainty (reflected in the lower real return) is more than the liquidity premium (reflected in a higher real return) required because the market for price-indexed instruments may be fairly illiquid.

Some advocates of price-indexed bonds suggest that if a government believes financial markets are underestimating its resolve to maintain price stability, issuing price-indexed securities should lead to lower government debt-servicing costs. Others maintain that because governments change regularly and tend not to have superior information about the path of inflation over the medium and longer terms, price-indexed instruments may be very costly to them. It is perhaps not surprising that some of the strongest advocates of price-indexed instruments have been the more independent central banks, which are arguably confident of maintaining price stability or low and stable rates of inflation.[11] These institutions believe that the issuance of price-indexed debt signals the government's anti-inflationary resolve and, by enhancing the credibility of monetary policy, helps lower inflationary expectations. When inflation risks are perceived to subside, the demand for such instruments declines.[12]

Many governments, however, have decided against issuing price-indexed bonds because they do not wish to bear the whole inflationary risk of unfavorable supply shocks and errors in monetary policy. They believe that price-indexed bonds contribute to inflationary expectations throughout the economy by signaling that the government sees inflation as inevitable. The introduction of these securities, in this view, would weaken the constituency for price stability and would be interpreted by wage and price setters as an attempt to create a more price-indexed economy. As a result, inflationary expectations would increase. Concern about raising inflationary expectations has been a major reason why some Latin American governments, including those of Argentina, Brazil, and Peru, have been reluctant to issue price-indexed debt. Other countries, such as Chile and Colombia, have issued price-indexed debt in order to obtain longer debt maturities and reduce the government's refinancing risk.

Some governments take the view that introducing price-indexed debt and floating-rate bonds with long maturities can provide a foundation for extending the yield curve for nominal bonds at a later stage. Others have worried that creating investor expectations for inflation protection will make it much more difficult to lengthen the yield curve for nominal debt instruments.

Issuance strategies

Even when corporate and subnational fixed-income markets are well developed, the central government is usually the dominant single issuer of securities in the domestic market. Governments tend to be aware that their fiscal and debt management strategies can markedly affect the trading performance of their domestic securities and the yields at which they are able to issue additional securities. This is especially true if a government were to issue domestic debt opportunistically and endeavor to generate income by trading government securities aggressively in the secondary market. While some investors might welcome the additional liquidity in the market that this could bring, others would be concerned about possible conflicts of interest between the government's proprietary trading and its role as issuer and regulator in the domestic financial market. They would assume that the government has an incentive to manipulate the market or to use inside information to gain pricing or trading advantages. Such concerns would quickly be reflected in higher interest rates if investors withdrew from the market or required higher bond yields (or lower bond prices) in order to invest.

For this reason, most OECD government debt managers have adopted domestic debt management practices aimed at reinforcing the government's reputation as a predictable and consistent issuer, committed to promoting competition among investors and ensuring a high degree of transparency regarding its decisionmaking. Few countries, for example, trade their debt in the secondary market except as part of normal liquidity management operations designed to smooth liquidity flows—e.g., through buying back illiquid debt issues or through switch offers that enable investors to transfer their holdings of illiquid bonds to new or more liquid benchmark issues.[13]

Among OECD countries, the principal stylized features of government issuance practices in treasury bill and bond markets can be briefly summarized. A combination of (mainly short-term) floating-rate debt and longer-term nominal bonds is issued, but the ratio of domestic floating-rate debt to total marketable domestic currency debt is generally below 35 percent, and below 15 percent when treasury bills are excluded.[14] Little or no long-maturity, floating-rate debt or foreign currency–linked domestic debt is issued (although some countries, including Australia, Canada, France, Greece, New Zealand, Sweden, the United Kingdom, and the United States, have introduced price-indexed bonds). Governments issue securities in a range of maturities in order to diversify their refinancing risk and create a yield curve of benchmark bonds that will serve as a pricing reference for other issuers and help investors assess credit risk.

Governments endeavor to reduce the liquidity risk premia in the yield curve for government bonds, and thereby lower their issuance costs, by committing to build the liquidity of their benchmark securities. With this objective in mind, they seek to limit the number of types of government bonds on issue and to restrict the proportion of nonmarketable debt that is issued. An excessive proliferation of government bonds on issue can segment or fragment the market and hinder the objective of building liquidity in a series of benchmark bonds. Private placement of nonmarketable bonds reduces the liquidity of the bond market and diminishes the transparency of government debt management.

In nearly all OECD countries, government bonds are sold through market-based auctions involving American- or Dutch-auction techniques.[15] Auctions are held regularly throughout the year in order to sample interest rates over time, thereby helping governments reduce the price risk that would otherwise be associated with the infrequent issuance of large volumes of debt.

A number of governments have committed to principles of transparency, predictability, and even-handedness in managing their domestic bond programs. They publish borrowing plans and auction dates well in advance and seek to be consistent in reviewing auction bids and in removing regulatory distortions that discriminate among investors. These governments believe that, over the medium term, adherence to these principles will lower their borrowing costs by reducing price uncertainty and encouraging competitive bidding and that the gains will outweigh any short-term advantages associated with an opportunistic domestic issuance strategy.[16]

To help manage their market risk, some governments have introduced callable bonds and domestic interest rate swaps. Callable government bonds attract lower prices from investors (and therefore require higher yields) than do noncallable bonds as they enable the government to call the bond and refinance when interest rates are low. The lower price bid by investors reflects the fact that they no longer own the option to hold these bonds to full maturity. Domestic interest rate swaps enable governments to alter the mix of fixed-rate and floating-rate debt. Governments have also introduced products to lower their debt-servicing costs. For example, strippable bonds attract a premium from investors who are seeking financial instruments that can be customized to meet their cash flow needs.

BUILDING DOMESTIC BOND MARKETS IN DEVELOPING COUNTRIES: SOME CONSIDERATIONS

Many emerging market governments find it difficult to extend the maturity of nominal fixed-income domestic currency bonds beyond two to three years. Limited demand for longer maturities may stem from a lack of institutional investors such as pension funds or life insurance companies, which normally require longer-term assets to manage their balance sheet risk. It may also reflect investor concerns about the government's creditworthiness as a result of a history of government default or a poor record in controlling government spending and creating a low-inflation environment. Investors may be reluctant to modify their inflationary expectations until the government's policy record improves substantially. Consequently, they may not be prepared to invest in longer-maturity debt or will do so only at yields that the government is unwilling to pay.

This situation creates difficult choices for a government. It could continue to issue short-maturity debt, but that would generate refinancing and interest rate risk. Issuing long-maturity floating-rate bonds can reduce refinancing risk, but the short duration of these instruments means exposure of the government's budgetary position to both nominal and real interest rate movements. Similarly, the government could issue long-maturity inflation-indexed debt, but it would bear the risk of adverse inflation.

If a government believes there is some demand for longer maturities or it anticipates large benefits, including externalities, from developing a domestic fixed-income market, it could simply decide to pay the higher debt-servicing costs associated with committing to extend the yield curve.

In doing so, it would need to consider the types of regulatory and institutional reform required to develop the absorptive capacity of this market. Alternatively, provided that concerns about debt sustainability and creditworthiness do not rule this out, a government could borrow in foreign currency—from the international financial intermediaries, where long-maturity debt at concessional rates is obtainable; from commercial banks, if that is possible; or by issuing bonds in the international capital market.[17] With each of these options, however, the government takes foreign exchange risk onto its balance sheet, and the lender bears the country credit risk on the securities. In short, high debt burdens and large financing needs invariably create difficult tradeoffs for governments.

In the OECD countries, the speed and sequence of the necessary institutional reforms and deregulation has varied. Progress has been heavily influenced by factors such as the initial state of the country's financial markets, the macroeconomic policy mix, and the soundness of bank balance sheets. Box 6 identifies some of the main, and generally applicable, elements of the market development programs implemented by OECD governments.

Box 6
Conditions for developing an efficient government securities market

In most OECD countries, the establishment of a government securities market has been pivotal in helping to create a liquid and efficient domestic debt market. Governments have adopted various approaches in the timing and sequencing of measures to develop these markets. An important prerequisite for building investor confidence is a record of a sound macroeconomic environment, including appropriate fiscal and monetary policies coupled with a viable balance of payments position and exchange rate regime.

In addition, developing a domestic securities market entails addressing, even in the nascent stages, securities market regulation, market infrastructure, the demand for securities, and the supply of securities. These elements, and the steps to be taken to support them, are discussed below.

Regulating the securities market. Early-stage measures include:

- Establishing a legal framework for securities issuance
- Creating a regulatory environment to foster market development and enable the enforcement of sound supervisory practices

- Introducing appropriate accounting, auditing, and disclosure practices for financial sector reporting.

Developing market infrastructure, to help build market liquidity and reduce systemic risk. Steps to be taken are as follows:

- Introducing trading arrangements, suitable for the size of the market, that include efficient and safe custody, clearing, and settlement procedures
- Encouraging the development of a system of market makers to enable buyers and sellers to transact efficiently at prices reflecting fair value
- Removing any tax or other regulatory impediments that may hamper trade in government securities
- Fostering, at a later stage, the scope for other money market and risk management instruments such as repos and interest rate futures and swaps.

Fostering demand for government securities. Strengthening demand involves acting on a broad front to build the potential investor base through measures such as:

- Removing regulatory distortions, which inhibit the development of institutional investors (e.g., carrying out pension reform)
- Eliminating below-market-rate funding through captive investor sources
- Implementing the appropriate regulatory regime and rules, which affect participation by foreign investors in the domestic market.

Building up the supply of government securities. The key measures for establishing an efficient primary market include:

- Establishing clear objectives for security issuance and debt management
- Developing projections of the government's liquidity needs
- Creating safe and efficient channels, targeted to investor needs, for the distribution of securities (e.g., auctions, syndication, and possible use of primary dealers), which will lower transaction costs
- Progressively extending the maturity of government securities
- Consolidating the number of debt issues and creating standardized securities with conventional maturities, with the aim of eventually providing market benchmarks
- Moving toward a predictable and transparent debt management operation, e.g., with preannounced issuance calendars and greater disclosure of funding needs and auction outcomes.

Source: World Bank and IMF 2001.

The macroeconomic foundation

Experiences with fostering the development of government bond and money markets in OECD countries and elsewhere demonstrate the importance of having in place a sound macroeconomic policy framework. Placing fixed-rate domestic currency government paper is extremely difficult if inflation is volatile and the government's fiscal deficit and its associated borrowing needs are very large. Investors focus on issues of fiscal sustainability and economic vulnerability and fear that unless substantial adjustments are made to spending or to effective tax rates, the government will face serious adverse debt-servicing spirals and will have greater incentive to default, through nonpayment or by permitting higher inflation to erode the real principal value of its outstanding bond commitments. Sound fiscal policy by itself, however, is not sufficient to prevent debt market crises from developing. Both Korea and Thailand were forecasting government fiscal surpluses before the onset of their financial market crisis in 1997, as was the Mexican government in 1995 prior to the *tesobono* crisis.

Deregulation

It is necessary to consider carefully the timing and sequencing of policy change in the area of capital account liberalization. Removing capital controls is one of the most powerful structural reforms that a government can undertake. It signals to domestic producers the need to become more competitive and to generate rates of return comparable to those of other world producers if they want to attract domestic and foreign savings. From a government debt management perspective, inflows of foreign capital into the government securities market broaden the government's investor base and can contribute to significant reductions in the government's borrowing costs. Nonresident ownership of government bonds in many OECD countries, for example, increased markedly as the removal of capital account restrictions was accelerated in the late 1980s and the 1990s.[18]

Capital account deregulation also imposes disciplines on economic policy more generally, given that investors can readily withdraw capital if the quality of economic management deteriorates. Sudden capital outflows can cause exchange rate pressures, interest rate pressures, or both, depending on the exchange rate regime in place. In many countries, the deregulation of domestic financial markets and the removal of controls on capital flows have not been supported by stable macroeconomic policies and sound prudential supervision and regulation. Some of these countries have experienced extensive financial disintermediation, very rapid growth of credit, asset price spirals, consequent deterioration in the quality of financial intermediaries' balance sheets, and banking crises (see, for example, Hausmann and Gavin 1995; Mishkin 1999).

Country experiences in Asia, Latin America, and elsewhere suggest that sound macroeconomic policy is necessary for successful financial sector deregulation and that the capital account should be opened gradually. Its opening should be preceded by substantial domestic financial market deregulation and the lowering of protective barriers in the tradables (export and import-substitution) sector. Significant deregulation of the domestic financial market is an important precondition if the government is to avoid sizeable outflows of domestic savings from savers who were previously heavily regulated. Without reductions in border protection (especially in quantitative restrictions) and in explicit and implicit government guarantees, there is a significant risk that foreign capital will flow into the more profitable protected sectors, particularly if the domestic market is large (see Edwards 1984). Country experience suggests that it may be wise to phase in the liberalization of capital flows by reducing controls on longer-term foreign direct investment before easing or removing controls on short-term financial inflows (see Eichengreen and others 1998). Foreign direct investment can increase an economy's productive potential, and it is likely to be much less volatile than short-term money market and speculative flows.

Prudential supervision

Equally important are an effective system of prudential supervision and the practice of prudent financial management by domestic banks and associated intermediaries. This can help reduce the risk of poor asset and liability management decisions by domestic institutions as their access to world capital markets increases and they have larger financial flows to manage. Under these changed conditions, poorly performing or insolvent banks have incentives to enter into transactions involving increased risk and higher expected returns. It is important that the problems associated with poorly performing, undercapitalized banks be addressed through such means as new capital injections and disinvestment, including closure. Often, it is necessary to change the management of the institutions in order to create an altered set of performance expectations.

Removal of distortions

It is important to review the tax regime and other regulatory policies and practices that could inhibit the development of domestic capital markets. Such policies may include, for example, regulations providing captive funding for the government by financial intermediaries at low interest rates; tax policies that distort investment by diverting it from financial assets into speculative, nonfinancial assets; and credit allocation practices and tax policies that discriminate among financial institutions and borrowers.

Institutional infrastructure

Governments should develop an institutional infrastructure that supports the growth of domestic capital markets. The removal of restrictions that inhibit the development of institutions that may be natural buyers of government securities, such as pension and retirement funds, insurance companies, banks, and mutual funds, may require a significant reexamination of the government's role. For example, governments should review their reasons for retaining ownership of particular financial institutions and should take steps to avoid conflicts of interest. In doing so, they should ensure the separation of responsibilities for government debt management and for asset allocation decisions in financial institutions such as government-owned pension funds, thereby enabling the latter to make their own asset allocation choices.[19]

Standards for domestic institutions

As part of the deregulation of the domestic financial market, disclosure and supervision requirements are needed to reduce the risk of institutions' being exposed to fraud or adopting imprudent asset and liability management practices that increase the risk of institutional insolvency or even of systemic failure in the financial system. Appropriate accounting and auditing standards and disclosure practices with respect to financial and corporate sector reporting should be introduced, along with well-designed systems of prudential supervision and regulation of domestic financial institutions.

Government actions to support domestic markets

Countries can benefit by adopting, as appropriate, sound government debt management practices used in other countries and by being consistent and even-handed in designing and implementing regulations. Governments can help build liquidity within the government bond market by reducing market fragmentation caused by issuance of an excessive variety of special-purpose bonds and by supporting the creation of liquid benchmark bonds and the development of repo markets. They can encourage secondary trading by removing impediments such as restrictions on the short-selling of bonds and by modifying accounting practices that hinder the trading of securities. In several emerging market countries, secondary market trading increased after commercial banks were required to mark parts of their portfolio to market.

Long-term commitment

Investors recognize that governments may not follow through on announced policy goals and that they may be tempted to reduce the annual debt-servicing costs recorded in their budget documentation by taking on foreign currency exposures or by resorting to punitive regulation to capture domestic savings. Investors also know that building a strong domestic financial market requires a long-term policy commitment, perseverance, and consistency in government policy setting and decisionmaking. They therefore look to governments to constantly reinforce their intention and commitment to support the development of a domestic financial market by addressing the issues discussed in this chapter and by employing borrowing practices that are geared toward improving the efficiency of the domestic market.

NOTES

1. In such a situation, governments might aim to meet their financing needs through other techniques, such as selling retail instruments or placing securities with a small number of institutions. Where a government has adopted a trading partner's currency as its domestic currency, the trading partner's capital market instruments could be used by local corporate bodies and households to manage their balance sheet risk.

2. The Australian government is currently considering some of these issues, since the government's ratio of net debt to GDP is around 5 percent and significant financial surpluses are projected. In the United States, before the federal government returned to fiscal deficits in 2002, the Congressional Budget Office was projecting zero net federal government debt by 2008.

3. Various policy issues that can arise in developing domestic bond markets are discussed more fully in World Bank and IMF (2001).

4. The benefits of establishing domestic bond markets and the policy issues that often arise in developing these markets are discussed in Turner (2003).

5. As discussed in chapter 4, bond financing helps the government avoid the deadweight costs associated with large and rapid increases in tax rates.

6. In a cross-country comparison of roughly a hundred countries over the period 1960–90, Barro (1998) found a negative relationship between inflation and growth in countries with an annual inflation rate of more than 20 percent. For inflation rates below 20 percent per year, the relationship between growth and inflation was not statistically significant.

7. These thoughts are fleshed out in greater detail and with country examples in Federal Reserve chairman Alan Greenspan's address, "Lessons from the Global Crises," presented at the program of seminars that preceded the 1999 World Bank–IMF Annual Meetings in Washington, D.C.

8. Sometimes these instruments are not tradable but may be redeemed at par plus interest.

9. An exception is Chile, where indexed bonds account for most of the domestic government debt. In Israel, such instruments represent 29 percent of the domestic government bonds on issue. Among OECD governments, the United Kingdom had the highest proportion of price-indexed bonds in its total outstanding domestic bonds in mid-2002, with 26 percent.

10. These issues are discussed further in chapters 2 and 4 and in Missale (1997).

11. The Reserve Bank of Australia, the Bank of Canada, the Bank of England, the Reserve Bank of New Zealand, and the U.S. Federal Reserve System have from time to time been strong supporters of price-indexed debt.

12. In 1999 the New Zealand government decided to discontinue the issuance of inflation-adjusted bonds.

13. Several European countries initiated a major switching program in the spring of 1999 in the context of the launch of new benchmark issues following the introduction of the euro.

14. Short-term floating-rate debt often takes the form of 3-month, 6-month, and 12-month treasury bills. Governments endeavor to establish a series of benchmark bonds in a range of maturities and often issue bonds with 3-, 5-, and 10-year maturities. In some economies, nominal bond

maturities extend to 30 years. Nominal bonds usually have a bullet structure but may also include zero-coupon bonds.

15. A reasonable number of participants in auctions (say, 10 or more) is needed to reduce the risk of collusion among bidders. Under a Dutch, or uniform price, auction, all successful bidders receive securities at the highest market-clearing price (or the lowest yield accepted). In an American, or discriminatory price, auction, successful bidders pay the price they bid.

16. An opportunistic strategy might mean issuing securities only when the government considers market demand to be strong, and it may involve targeting individual investors or groups of investors. For example, Denmark's Nationalbanken issues all its government bonds and Treasury notes through a tap mechanism rather than through an auction program. The Danish authorities believe that when there is a need to borrow and markets are favorable, a presence in the market avoids creation or amplification of negative market trends. Details of the previous day's sales of government securities by the Nationalbanken are published daily.

17. The volume of foreign currency bond issuance tends to contract when credit spreads exceed 700 basis points over the government benchmark comparator (e.g., U.S. Treasuries for dollar transactions). This is because investors are concerned about the country credit risk, and borrowers seek to avoid high debt-servicing costs in foreign currency.

18. In late 2002, nonresident ownership of domestic government bonds was 63 percent in Ireland, 60 percent in Belgium, and 41 percent in Spain and Sweden. In the mid-1990s, the proportion of foreign ownership reached 75 percent in New Zealand.

19. South Africa, for example, separated the responsibility for debt management and for government pension fund management at an early stage. This freed the government pension fund to make its own decisions on asset allocation.

Chapter 10

Building Capability
in Government
Debt Management

Since the late 1980s, upgrading the professionalism of government debt management has been an important policy objective for many countries. Although some capacity building has taken place in the course of broader governance reforms aimed at enhancing the productivity and effectiveness of the public sector, much of it has been motivated by the rapid accumulation of debt and the need to manage the associated risks to the government's balance sheet, or by the need to respond to the opportunities and risks associated with financial market deregulation and the product innovation that accompanies it.

This chapter explores some of the issues involved in building capacity in government debt management in developing and emerging market countries. Two stylized country situations are then discussed. In the first, the domestic debt market is largely underdeveloped, government debt management objectives and accountabilities are not well specified, and the manual debt-recording system provides poor-quality information. The priority for this country is to improve the basic debt management system and promote domestic debt markets. In the second example, both the domestic money and bond markets and the debt management office are more sophisticated, and the task is to develop a risk management capability.

CONDITIONS FOR SUCCESSFUL CAPACITY BUILDING

All governments that have successfully built up their debt management capacity have begun by defining their debt management objectives and their tolerance for risk. They have decided which parts of the government balance sheet the government's debt managers should be accountable for and what type of governance and institutional framework is best suited to meeting their objectives. The process is the same for the U.S. government as for any highly indebted poor country.

A country's needs for capacity building in government debt management are shaped by its unique circumstances. Important considerations are the current and projected size of the government's debt portfolio and the nature of the risks associated with it; the quality of the government's macro-economic and regulatory policies and debt management; the government's sovereign credit rating (or, if the government is not rated by the international sovereign credit rating agencies, the financial markets' assessment of its creditworthiness); the quality of public sector financial management throughout the government; and institutional capacity within the government to design and implement public sector management reforms.

Despite differences among countries, government debt managers are in general agreement as to what constitutes prudent debt management.[1] There is a broad consensus that it is essential to:

- Set transparent objectives for government debt management and establish a legislative framework that clarifies roles and accountabilities for financial management in the public sector and for debt management in particular.

- Ensure that government debt management is conducted within a supportive macroeconomic policy environment. This may entail establishing limits or constraints on government debt expansion and separating decisionmaking responsibilities for debt management policy and for monetary policy. (Alternatively, if a complete separation between debt management and monetary policy management is not possible, arrangements may be made for coordinating and sharing information between debt managers and the central bank, particularly with respect to the government's cash management.)

- Build a sound institutional structure that includes skilled staff, accurate and reliable management information systems, and delegation of responsibilities and associated accountabilities to the various government agencies involved in debt management.

- Identify the key portfolio-related risks, particularly those stemming from overreliance on foreign currency debt instruments, and the refinancing and budgetary risks associated with having large amounts of short-term debt that has to be rolled over frequently.

Among the prerequisites for successful reform are agreement among advisers and policymakers concerning the policy challenges and operational risks associated with the government's debt management, and a strong political commitment to addressing them. The main stages of the implementation process must be clearly understood, and realistic timeframes and budgets have to be established. A common mistake is to underestimate the magnitude of the resources needed for successful capacity building, the time required, and the budgetary costs involved, especially in acquiring or developing skilled staff and installing satisfactory management information systems.

Resources and staffing

Government recognition that building a debt management capability is an important policy priority must be accompanied by provision of adequate resources. Debt management reforms often fail because funding for hiring skilled staff, for training, and for systems investments is inadequate and inconsistent with the stated goals. Often, however, the binding resource constraint is not a financial one but an overall scarcity of financial specialists with market experience and of managers with the necessary skills to guide the capacity-building process. In some cases, more flexible public sector labor market or contracting procedures may have to be adopted in order to recruit qualified staff and managers. Some governments have tried to address this issue by seconding staff from state-owned entities and the private sector or by recruiting overseas. These strategies have helped governments initiate capacity-building projects and complete specific tasks, but they should be accompanied by transfer of skills and technology to local staff. Otherwise, capacity building can stagnate or be reversed, should the contracts or secondment arrangements not be renewed.

Organizational arrangements

On the organizational front, there is a common tendency to conclude, prematurely and often erroneously, that the most desirable institutional solution is to establish an autonomous government debt management office, with its own board of directors or an advisory board, as a state-owned enterprise outside the ministry of finance. This preference is often driven by difficulties with attracting and retaining skilled, experienced staff because salaries are not competitive with those in the private sector, but it is sometimes motivated by the proponents' desire to be part of such an organizational structure.

Regardless of the institutional arrangements for government debt management, building capacity in public debt management is a long-term endeavor, the success of which will require all the management skills necessary for successful change management. Existing organizational arrangements, with public debt management functions perhaps spread among departments or located in the central bank, may have been in place for decades. Strong leadership may well be needed to overcome possible resistance to proposals to reformulate debt management responsibilities.

Time required

Programs aimed at developing a sound government debt management capability can take many years. This is especially true where substantial data-cleaning and systems development work is involved, where debt management policy and monetary policy are closely interwoven, where the quality of government cash management is poor, and where government debt managers have a broad mandate that extends to promoting the development of the domestic bond market. Even as capacity building is proceeding, debt managers still have to carry out their core responsibilities. Programs substantially upgrading the quality of debt management in many OECD countries during the late 1980s and early 1990s often took five years or longer, given the challenges of recruiting and training staff, developing a risk management strategy, and supporting it with appropriate management information systems and documentation on policies and procedures. Comprehensive reform can take a decade or more when initial conditions are much less supportive than those prevailing in many OECD countries at the start of their programs.

Complementary institutional and policy reforms

Measures to improve debt management capability need to be complemented and supported by other public sector reforms. Upgrading the quality of government debt management requires institutional changes in other areas of the ministry of finance (e.g., those involved with budget forecasts, preparation of financial accounts, and monitoring and analysis of spending and revenue trends in government agencies), as well as elsewhere in the government. Successful development of government cash management procedures, for example, usually requires improvements in forecasting and other financial management skills within the ministry of finance and in other government departments. Changes in liquidity forecasting practices at the central bank or in the way in which this information is received and processed may be needed, as well.

Success also depends on the quality of the economic policy environment, particularly with respect to fiscal and monetary policy and financial sector deregulation. Debt management reforms take longer and are more complex when undertaken against a backdrop of poor macroeconomic policy and limited financial market deregulation. It is very difficult, for example, to sustain momentum on a program to upgrade the quality of government debt management if the government's debt managers have to concentrate most of their effort on meeting government funding demands stemming from poor fiscal policy. Similarly, several countries, especially in Latin America, have had difficulty in establishing domestic bond markets and lengthening the government yield curve because of a history of macroeconomic policy imbalances, including large fiscal deficits and high and variable inflation, and of previous defaults on government debt obligations.

CARRYING OUT A CAPACITY-BUILDING PROGRAM

The sequencing of the stages of capacity building will differ among countries depending on the initial state of government debt management and the policy and institutional factors described in the preceding section. The preliminary assessment should be followed up by decisions on debt management goals, the legal framework, the responsibilities of debt managers, staffing, the debt-recording and management information systems to be used, and whether to develop risk management capability.

Initial assessment

Capacity building begins with a sound diagnosis of the existing arrangements for debt management that assesses the strengths, vulnerabilities, and risks of the government's debt management and, where relevant, the state of development of the government securities market. The diagnosis should review areas such as debt management objectives, the governance and legal framework surrounding public debt management, institutional arrangements relating to individual debt management functions, the debt management strategy and the risk management framework, the relationship between debt management policy and monetary and fiscal policies, and issues such as contingent liabilities and the borrowing and risk management practices of state-owned enterprises as they affect government debt management. It should also cover the operational risks in government debt management and the adequacy of management information systems, staff capacity, and training programs. On the portfolio management side, the diagnosis should assess the main cost- and risk-related features of the government's debt portfolio, such as the extent to which maturities are bunched, the type of currency exposures in the portfolio and the rationale for having them, the sensitivity of debt-servicing expenditures to changes in exchange rates and interest rates, the amount of liquidity on hand at any time, and how the liquidity is managed. The assessment should indicate the scope for reducing risk, improving efficiency, and reducing costs through debt management reform and should outline the key stages of a project implementation plan.

Examination of the reasons behind the need to borrow is important. Borrowing might be required to refinance existing debt, fund the government's budget deficits, cover government contingent liabilities falling due or, if the government has a fixed exchange rate, to finance the foreign exchange reserves needed to support the private sector's demand for foreign currency. Strains on fiscal policy may arise from, for example, a lack of fiscal discipline among ministers, corruption, poorly targeted spending, inadequate expenditure control policies, adverse debt-servicing spirals, inefficient tax policies (including tax expenditures), and ineffective revenue collection processes.[2] These factors may require the government to run large primary surpluses in order to prevent an unsustainable build up in government indebtedness. Deteriorating fiscal positions and the growth in credit creation that often accompanies them can result in excessive growth in aggregate demand, which in turn can lead to widening external imbalances and additional foreign exchange borrowing to replenish the government's foreign currency reserves.

Goal setting

Once the diagnosis of debt management and macroeconomic policies has been completed, government debt managers should endeavor to set sound goals for the government's debt portfolio as regards cost and risk and any other important public policy objectives, such as promoting the development of a domestic bond market. This should assist the debt managers in making such decisions as whether to borrow in local or foreign currency, what maturities to aim for, and whether to issue fixed-rate or floating-rate debt.

Legal framework for debt management

The legal authorities necessary to support government debt management should be reviewed (and modified where necessary) to ensure that the legal framework is sound; the accountabilities with respect to debt management decision making, advisory, and processing roles are clear; and the institutional framework is both efficient and conducive to the rapid sharing of information. Review of the legal authorizations underpinning key debt management decisions and the way they are applied should help identify areas of duplication and tension and determine whether monitoring and control procedures are effective.

Decisions on responsibilities of debt managers

At an early stage, decisions will probably have to be made on the debt managers' responsibilities with respect to the debt portfolios of state-owned enterprises and the management of contingent liabilities. Before deciding whether to assign any responsibilities in these areas to government debt managers, it is important to make substantial progress on governance procedures relating to the central government's debt and to demonstrate sound performance in the management of this portfolio. Having to take on the management of contingent liabilities and, possibly, the debt of state-owned enterprises at the outset could seriously overburden the debt managers and slow the core development program.

Within the central government debt management function, decisions will need to be made about the debt managers' responsibilities with regard to the types of government cash management discussed in chapter 2. At a minimum, the government needs robust forecasts of its spending and revenue flows throughout the year in order to determine whether the domestic borrowing program should be adjusted in response to changes in fiscal flows—for example, by canceling a projected issuance or by conducting further sales of securities. It also needs to know the daily projected net injection into or withdrawal from the banking system as a result of government financial operations.

Usually the responsibility for forecasting departmental cash flows is a core Ministry of Finance function and requires skilled accounting staff across government and an efficient accounting system. This information is made available to the debt managers on a regular (usually daily) basis. It is unusual for the debt managers to be assigned this forecasting responsibility, although they may undertake their own forecasting based on previous years' expenditure and revenue patterns as a consistency check. At a minimum, the debt managers should understand how the data are derived and be confident that procedures and accountabilities are acceptable and that the quality of the cash forecasting (assessed by comparing actual cash positions with the forecasts) is reasonable.

The debt managers should be consulted on the design of departmental cash management incentives and the operating procedures and sanctions that could be applied to improve the quality of cash forecasting in government departments. On the transactions side, the central bank may be better equipped than the government debt managers to undertake liquidity-smoothing operations on behalf of the government. If the central bank becomes the agent for these transactions, it is essential that the ministry of finance retain responsibility for setting the policy framework guiding decisions on quantities and pricing.

Staffing

Staff members who undertake portfolio transactions, including new borrowing, need to have some market expertise and to understand the main market conventions so that they can assess the pricing and risks associated with transactions. Because staff with these qualifications can be difficult to find within the finance ministry, many developing countries prefer that the central bank (which often has more personnel with capital market experience) handle foreign currency borrowing until the necessary skills are available within the ministry. (This was the route taken in Brazil and Thailand.) Alternatively, it may be feasible to have central bank staff transfer to the ministry of finance, if compensation, pension, and other career-related issues can be resolved. Some staff with risk management skills are also needed to undertake risk analysis and to monitor and report on the management of risks in the portfolio. At an early stage, this group would begin designing portfolio management guidelines and policies for the office. People who are trained to operate a debt-recording system and to settle and account for transactions are also required, as are skilled legal staff (see box 7).

Box 7
Building human resource capacity for government debt
management: New Zealand's approach

The New Zealand Debt Management Office (NZDMO) has a development program designed to build the professional and personal skills of staff members. The program is reviewed and monitored regularly. Training programs, conducted by external suppliers or provided through on-the-job mentoring, are used extensively to build skills in all aspects of debt management, including governance practices and portfolio and risk management. There are extensive opportunities for part-time study or for enrolling in chartered financial analyst (CFA) courses, with the NZDMO paying the fees and providing time off for study. When experts have been hired, their contracts place considerable emphasis on training other staff.

New staff generally require the most development and typically receive a greater proportion of the training opportunities. This has become an important factor in attracting applicants to the NZDMO. Although staff are not formally bonded as a result of the training, the organization has had low staff turnover. Other recruitment practices, particularly the ability to offer close to market rates, allow experienced people to be recruited to add depth to the team.

The quality of the work programs and training are key factors in attracting and retaining staff. The work program includes opportunities to advise on the design and implementation of debt management strategy, the development of the domestic debt market, the management of contingent liabilities, and the interplay between debt management policy and monetary and fiscal policy. Valuable learning opportunities arise from networking with investors, other financial institutions, and rating agencies, and participating in conferences and publishing research papers. The technical expertise gained can also assist career development in that it is valued by state-owned enterprises and the private sector.

Choice of debt-recording and management information systems

Systems decisions represent a critical stage in the capacity-building process. Reliable debt-recording systems are essential, for the reasons discussed in chapter 8. The purchase and installation of new systems can take several years, depending on the amount of customization involved, and building a management information system in-house can take considerably longer. Often, simply to maintain momentum in the capacity-building process, there is a tendency to rush into a buy-or-build decision before an adequate analysis has been made of systems needs and the best way of addressing them. This can demoralize and disempower the users and systems analysts and lead to considerable financial cost if incorrect judgments are made. Regardless of the type of system selected, it is important to have an open architecture and to avoid data redundancy.

Assessment of the need for risk management capacity

Whether to establish a risk management office at an early stage depends on the size and riskiness of the government's debt portfolio. If the portfolio contains a great deal of foreign currency debt, with embedded optionality as a result of previous borrowing strategies, or contains large amounts of short-term domestic currency debt, the debt managers should endeavor to develop a risk management capacity early on. Some of the key steps in doing so are discussed in the second example in the next section.

TWO COUNTRY SCENARIOS

This section illustrates some of the issues discussed above by looking at capacity-building needs in two hypothetical country scenarios.

Case 1: Improving the debt management setting and moving toward computerized systems

In the first of the two country examples, the domestic debt market is largely underdeveloped, and the government meets its financing needs through donor funding, by borrowing from the multilateral development banks, and by issuing short-maturity domestic treasury notes or bills to captive institutions. Government debt management objectives and accountabilities are poorly specified, implementation functions are spread over several government agencies, and the manual debt-recording system provides poor-quality information.

Poorly performing manual debt-recording systems are often a symptom of broader organizational problems, such as inadequately defined goals and functions and unclear decisionmaking authorities and accountabilities. In developing countries, the incentives to share information among the various parties involved in government debt management are often weak because of disagreements over roles and decision making powers, inadequate systems of checks and balances, and difficulties in establishing accountability for quality assurance in such environments. These problems may be compounded by a shortage of well-trained staff and by low morale, both of which increase operating risk. Corruption or fraud can be a complicating factor.

There is little point in considering possible systems enhancements, such as the introduction of a computerized debt-recording system, until the data quality and organizational issues are resolved. An important initial step is to undertake a thorough audit of the quality of the loan data and to verify why data are unavailable or of poor quality. This requires an examination of all the business procedures involved in raising and disbursing loans, including arrangements for initiating borrowing requests, depositing loan receipts, disbursing funds to end-users, on-lending, and making debt-servicing payments and principal repayments. Procedures for requesting and approving guarantees should also be reviewed.

It is important to "clean" the loan accounting data and to retrieve missing information on cash flow obligations. This process can take several months, and multilateral development banks and other lenders may have to be approached for information on cash flows and compliance arrangements. A repository for all loan documentation should be established, and records relating to borrowing, disbursement, on-lending, and guarantees should be centralized.

These steps often need to be accompanied by measures to remedy inefficient or dysfunctional organizational behavior. In endeavoring to resolve these issues, the government should ensure that its debt management objectives are clearly expressed and are well understood by debt management officials. An unambiguous assignment of responsibilities and accountabilities is needed, along with strong management, if tensions are to be resolved within the ministry of finance—let alone among the different government agencies that the ministry might interact with, such as the central bank, the government planning commission, the ministry of international cooperation, and the ministry of justice. Within the ministry of finance, several departments may be involved, and in some countries requests for debt management information can take several months to be answered. Unless these agency costs are addressed, the development of professional debt management practices will be impossible.

In drawing up its debt management objectives, the government should specify its risk tolerance or its degree of risk aversion. Given the quality of the loan portfolio data and the limited number of trained staff, the managers responsible for reviewing the government's debt may not be able to undertake the scenario analysis outlined in chapter 4, but it is still possible to make judgments about the preferred degree of refinancing risk and the volatility of debt-servicing costs. An examination of fundamental economic relationships can help guide initial benchmarking decisions (as discussed in chapter 7) or can be used in identifying the main currencies in which the government should seek to borrow. Decisions in these areas are important because borrowers have choices with respect to maturity, currency, and interest rate basis in negotiating loan terms with most multilateral lending institutions, and many bilateral donors also offer options regarding maturity and interest rate basis.

Making policy decisions in these areas, however, is meaningless if the desire or capacity to implement them is lacking. To illustrate, Nigeria's government debt management strategies often had little impact on the government's debt situation because legislation on borrowing policy was not rigorously enforced and did not guide government borrowing decisions. For many years, the country operated without full knowledge of the government's foreign currency debt obligations.[3]

A key organizational step is to concentrate the arrangements for sovereign debt management. This usually means centralizing operational responsibility (other than some roles that might be implemented more effectively in the central bank) in the ministry of finance rather than spreading them over several government agencies. It also entails rationalization of the involvement of various groups within the ministry of finance. No matter what operational procedures are introduced, responsibility for debt management policy should rest with the ministry of finance. As discussed in chapter 3, these authorities and accountabilities need to be supported by clear delegations.

Where developing a domestic debt market is both feasible and efficient, the government should begin to do so (see chapter 9). As capital market conditions and organizational competencies permit, the government should explore ways to separate debt management policy and monetary policy, as outlined in chapter 2.

Once the data problems have been resolved and key organizational challenges have been addressed, a computerized debt-recording system can be introduced. Most emerging market governments have adopted the

UNCTAD or the Commonwealth Secretariat debt-recording system (DMFAS and CR-DRMS, respectively) rather than develop their own (for the reasons outlined in chapter 8).[4] Both systems are electronically linked to the World Bank's debt sustainability software and Debt Recording System (DRS).[5] They provide countries with a comprehensive debt-recording capability and enable them to simulate the effects of various debt-servicing scenarios. UNCTAD is now co-owner of the Debt Sustainability Model (DSM+) developed by the World Bank and has integrated the DSM+ into the DMFAS.

Case 2: Developing a middle-office capability

In the second example, domestic money markets and government bond markets are more developed, responsibility for government debt management is centralized within the government, and a computerized debt-recording system with a consolidated database functions efficiently. The main challenge here is to develop a risk management office, or middle office.

Between two World Bank surveys, in 1997 and 1999, of 48 IBRD borrowing countries, the number of those that had adopted strategic benchmarks for the government's foreign currency portfolio increased from 2 to 10. Among these 10 countries, only one, Colombia, had developed a middle office (see box 8). Most of the 48 countries had computerized

---

Box 8
Strengthening middle-office capacity: the case of Colombia

In the mid-1990s Colombia undertook a project for improving its public debt management capacity. The project, which was partly financed by the World Bank and the Corporación Andina de Fomento, involved the debt management office of the Ministry of Finance (the General Directorate of Public Credit) and the state entities with the most significant proportions of foreign currency debt. The project had the strong backing of the minister and vice-minister of finance and the director general of public credit.

Important debt management institutional elements were already in place, including a consolidated debt management office responsible for both domestic currency and foreign currency debt. A computerized debt

(Box continues on the following page.)

Box 8 (continued)

database, albeit with many technical problems, had been introduced, and the front office had begun tapping international capital markets. An investment-grade rating facilitated the front office's placement of funds abroad with relatively long maturities.

The debt office accelerated its work on developing the government domestic debt market after the central bank law of 1993 prevented the central bank from lending to the government. However the debt office faced many challenges, including very substantial refinancing risk given the short maturity of the domestic debt, growing currency and interest rate risk, and the continuing issuance of government guarantees to the private sector.

A key problem in establishing the middle office was to overcome low civil service salaries and high staff turnover. Several technical staff were hired at specially established salary levels or as consultants.

The project took several years to implement. Various modules were developed simultaneously so that work could continue on one or more fronts if constraints developed.

Many important objectives were achieved, including:

- Implementation of methodologies for risk quantification of the foreign currency debt benchmark.
- Design of a foreign currency debt benchmark, which was approved by the minister of finance.
- Establishment of a debt management committee to periodically analyze the debt management strategy and its implementation. The committee included the minister and deputy ministers of finance, the head of the debt management office, and the treasurer. The central bank's head of monetary operations and head of international reserves were also invited to join.
- Implementation of the foreign currency benchmarking strategy through new debt issuance, swaps, and buybacks.
- Creation of a postgraduate program in public debt management in cooperation with a local university and development of extensive training programs.

In parallel, another debt management unit developed a methodology for quantifying guarantees extended by the central and subnational governments to private sector infrastructure projects. This was successfully incorporated into a law that established a special fund for budgeting the expected cost of the guarantees.

debt-recording systems, and many indicated that they were interested in establishing a middle office. Only 3 of the 48 IBRD borrowing countries attending the World Bank sovereign debt management forum in November 1999 had portfolio risk management systems technology.

Whether a separate middle-office capability is needed depends on the nature of the portfolio risk and the operational risks within the debt management unit. If the portfolio contains only domestic currency debt, if derivatives are not used by the debt managers, and if there is no tactical risk taking, sophisticated risk analysis may not be necessary. Simple cash flow simulations could be used to help analyze the cost-risk tradeoff of different debt structures (e.g., different mixes of fixed- and floating-rate debt) and to arrive at a duration benchmark. Alternatively, an overall portfolio structure could be derived by ensuring that the maturity schedule for new debt spreads repayment commitments over several years, and that liquidity is built up in those benchmark bond issues for which investor demand is strongest. In order to prevent excessive refinancing risk, it is sensible to set limits on the amount of outstanding debt rolling over in any single year.

Still, because the level and volatility of debt-servicing costs can have important effects on the budget and on fiscal indicators, a consolidated strategy for managing the cost and risk of the total portfolio of government debt should be developed. In the countries with the most advanced debt management practices, responsibility for formulating this strategy and for ensuring compliance with it is usually assigned to the middle office.

Building a sound risk management capability within a sovereign debt management operation can take several years, as it did in Belgium, Colombia, Finland, Ireland, New Zealand, and Sweden. How countries should begin this process is a question to which there is no uniform answer, but the following considerations are relevant.

In developing a middle-office capacity, government debt managers need to know for which part of the government balance sheet they are accountable. For example, will they be required to undertake borrowing for state-owned enterprises and manage the balance sheet risks for them, and if so, how? Will there be guidelines for the borrowing and risk management activities of the state-owned enterprises, and will those guidelines cover domestic as well as foreign currency transactions? Will the debt managers be expected to derive a foreign currency benchmark for these entities, as in Colombia? Will they have a specific role in monitoring contingent liabilities, managing their risk, pricing and structuring new obligations, and so on? All these issues affect the functions of the middle office and the systems and analytical capacity that need to be developed.

Given the challenges involved in building up skills and establishing suitable systems for a middle office, governments are probably better off first developing a strong risk management capability for a central government debt portfolio rather than expanding into broader public sector portfolio management at an early stage. An initial approach with respect to state-owned enterprises might be to establish general guidelines for their borrowing or portfolio risk management and to begin monitoring, rather than directly managing, the risks associated with contingent liabilities.

A clear mandate for the role, functions, and deliverables expected of the middle office should be prepared once an assessment has been made of the main types of risk that need to be managed. In assessing market risk, government debt managers could undertake some of the types of risk analysis discussed in chapters 4, 5, and 7. Often, a helpful starting point is to use scenario analysis to explore the sensitivity of debt-servicing projections to different interest rate and exchange rate scenarios, assuming various currency compositions and interest rate structures for the government's debt. This enables an analysis of the cost and risk tradeoffs associated with different debt structures. After a preferred debt structure has been identified, a strategic benchmark can be developed and, as outlined in chapter 7, can be used to ensure that all portfolio decisions are consistent with the government's cost and risk preferences.

This analysis should also prepare the way for work on compiling a portfolio management policy that specifies the policies and procedures for managing all portfolio-related risks. Liquidity risk, refinancing risk, and credit risk (relating to the management of foreign currency liquidity or the existence of swaps) require special attention, as deficiencies in these areas can result in technical default. Governments should not, for example, be forced to confront possible default because of credit policies that are based on poor judgment, or because debt managers have created unacceptable levels of refinancing risk. For most countries, credit risk can be readily managed by limiting the types of credit exposure entered into and by introducing the types of measures outlined in chapter 5. At the same time, governments can endeavor to reduce their refinancing risk by taking advantage of the flexibility in repayment terms offered by some multilateral lending institutions, paying higher debt-servicing costs on new public issues to secure longer-maturity funding, or targeting new issuance to fill gaps in the maturity profile of the portfolio.

Regardless of whether the responsibilities of the middle office match the set of functions described in chapter 3, it is essential that the monitoring, compliance, and control functions of that office be respected from the time it is established. Setting up a middle office can create tension within the portfolio management team, which may previously have had greater control over portfolio management decisions and whose performance may in the past have been less intensively scrutinized. This tension can lead to difficulties between front-office and middle-office staff—for example, if the portfolio management team pressures the middle office to set benchmarks or introduce performance measurement systems that will make future front-office performance look very favorable. Equally, a heavy-handed approach to risk management strategy may demotivate the portfolio management team and reduce its creativity in searching for ways to add value. Middle-office and front-office teams work best when there is a good understanding of the roles of each group and regular communication concerning work programs and performance.

Finding suitable staff is often the most difficult step. Risk analysis requires staff who are well trained in modern financial theory and mathematics and who, ideally, have a good understanding of macroeconomic relationships and the considerations that drive sound public policy. Because such skills command a high value in the private sector, civil service salary scales can make it difficult to recruit and retain staff. A strategy for developing risk analysis competency may involve seconding staff from the central bank, hiring long-term consultants, or establishing skill- or performance-based salary structures. A continuous training and evaluation program is also necessary, particularly when the strategy involves hiring young staff and training them in finance. Regardless of the recruiting and training strategy adopted, overcoming the skills constraint is likely to be expensive and time consuming, and policies need to be in place to retain these staff, given their obvious marketability.[6]

Middle offices function best when they are an integral part of the debt management operation. The middle office should not be set up as an independent office outside the debt management unit because it has to be able to carry on day-to-day coordination with front- and back-office staff and with the head of the debt management unit. The normal practice is to make the middle office part of a debt management unit within the ministry of finance or part of a separate debt management agency located outside the ministry of finance and reporting directly to the minister of finance. It is unusual to locate a debt management middle office in the central bank, although the bank may itself have a middle office supporting its management of foreign exchange reserves. Locating the debt management function in the central bank could conflict with the central bank's monetary policy responsibilities and risk diminishing its independence.

Risk analysis requires a consolidated database for the domestic and foreign-currency debt portfolios and a system capable of providing debt-servicing projections based on assumptions about future funding needs, the types of debt to be issued, and future interest rates and exchange rates. Ideally, the system should have an open architecture capable of being linked to other analytical models to enable more sophisticated risk analysis.

A decision on whether to introduce specialized risk management software should be deferred until risk management skills within the office have been built up and a sound technical understanding of the risk management alternatives has been acquired. Otherwise, important decisions relating to the establishment of a risk management framework may be made without a full understanding of alternative strategies or of which software is most appropriate.[7] "Model risk" can be very significant, and debt managers should be cautious about rushing into decisions to purchase the expensive risk management software that has come onto the market in recent years. Much of this software is aimed at asset managers who actively trade large portfolios. There is also the question of the compatibility of such software with existing management information systems within the debt office. Decisions as to whether to buy or build a risk management model should be guided by the considerations set forth in chapter 8.

Within the debt management operation, middle-office staff should work closely with the front office to explore ways of improving the efficiency of the domestic fixed-income market in order to lower borrowing costs. As discussed in chapter 9, reforms in this area are particularly important because they have the potential to significantly reduce the government's balance sheet risk.

NOTES

1. Many of these issues are identified in "Guidelines for Public Debt Management" (World Bank and IMF 2001), which was prepared at the request of the International Monetary and Finance Committee (IMFC).

2. Tax expenditures are tax allowances and credits, such as mortgage interest deductions and capital expenditure allowances, that are designed to encourage certain activities without apparent government expenditure. They necessitate higher tax rates than would otherwise be necessary and lead to distortions in factor markets.

3. Nigeria's government debt management practices are described in an April 2000 draft study, "Debt Management in African Countries," prepared for the African Development Bank. See also Okonjo-Iweala, Soludo, and Muhtar 2003.

4. About 100 countries currently use the DMFAS or the CS-DRMS.

5. The DRS provides an alternative source of country data, drawing on an extensive external debt database. The DSM+ helps borrowers quantify their financing needs under various macroeconomic assumptions.

6. Some debt management offices have been able to hold onto their staff because of their reputation as centers of excellence and their career development programs. The incentives of attractive training programs and professionally rewarding jobs have in some instances been complemented by specific measures to mitigate the risk of high staff turnover. Staff that have benefited from financial support for extensive training are often contracted to stay in the debt management office for specific periods.

7. Some countries joining the European Union, for example, purchased expensive risk management software before fully understanding their own needs.

Glossary

Active management: The pursuit of excess returns on a risk adjusted basis (or investment returns in excess of a specified benchmark).

Agency costs: The costs brought about by dysfunctional behavior within an agency because of poor governance and management practices (including costs created by conflicts of interest between shareholders, bondholders and managers).

Amortizing loan: A loan that is repaid by a number of periodic payments of principal, rather than by one payment at final maturity.

Arbitrage: Risk free returns made by simultaneously buying and selling a security at different prices in different markets.

Asset-and-Liability Management: This term embraces a range of risk management techniques designed to look at an entity's asset and liability portfolios in combination, with a view to reducing the effect of market related volatility on the entity's balance sheet.

Basis point: One hundredth of a percentage point of yield on a bond. A percentage point of yield is equivalent to 100 basis points.

Basis swap: A swap which entails both parties paying a floating rate, with the respective payments based on different indices.

Barbell strategy: A fixed-income strategy where the maturity of the securities are concentrated at two extremes.

Benchmark bond: Refers to a bond whose yield is reflected in the yield curve (and is often a specific maturity class, e.g., 5-year, 10-year, 30-year maturity) and because it is issued in large volume and is actively traded, it provides a standard for comparing the performance of other bonds.

Benchmark portfolio: A portfolio of securities which is used for comparing the performance of another portfolio. Benchmark portfolios are based on published indexes or may be customized for a particular investment strategy.

Bullet loan: A loan whose principal is payable in a single installment at maturity.

Buy and hold strategy: An investment strategy where the securities are retained throughout the investment period.

Call Options: A contract which the purchaser has the right to purchase underlying securities at a specified price over a defined time period. American-style options can be exercised at any time prior to their expiration date. European-style options can only be exercised during a specified period of time.

Cap: To set an upper limit on the interest rate to be paid.

Cash flow risk: Arises when differences in the timing of earnings and debt service may leave a debtor with insufficient cash flows to make loan repayments at certain points in time. Also called liquidity risk.

Collar: To set an upper limit ("Cap") and a lower limit ("Floor") on the interest rate to be paid, in order to reduce the cost of capping the interest rate.

Collateral: Assets pledged by a borrower to secure a transaction and which are subject to seizure in the event of default.

Commodity hedge: A financial instrument whose cash flows are linked or indexed to the price of a commodity.

Contagion: The transmission of economic and financial shocks to other countries or the cross-country correlation beyond fundamental linkages among the countries and beyond common shocks.

Cost at Risk: An analytical approach aimed at identifying the risk of an increase in government debt servicing costs based on market rate scenarios and probability distributions of future changes in market rates.

Credit risk: Arises when loan terms may not be appropriate for the borrower's debt servicing capacity, increasing the risk that the borrower cannot repay the loan.

Cross-Currency risk: Arises when the currency a debtor owes is different from the currency it earns.

Crowding out: A situation where excessive levels of government borrowing causes domestic interest rates to rise (and possibly the exchange rate), forcing other borrowers to defer investing or to seek more expensive or riskier sources of finance.

Currency swap: A financial transaction between two parties to exchange a series of interest and/or principal payments, thereby changing the underlying currency of denomination of an asset or a liability. A currency swap resembles a back-to-back or parallel loan involving two currencies.

Deadweight losses: The net loss in economic welfare (defined as the total losses to those who lose, minus the total gains to those who benefit) as a result of distortions to behavior caused by government intervention in competitive markets.

Default Risk: The risk that payment obligations will not be met on time.

Defeasance: A practice whereby the borrower sets aside cash or other financial assets which fully offsets the borrower's debt. In such situations, the borrower's debt and the offsetting cash or assets are removed from the balance sheet.

Derivative: A security, such as a swap, option, or future contract, whose value depends on the performance of the underlying instrument or asset (e.g., a bond, commodity, or equity).

Duration: The present value weighted time to maturity of the cash flows of a bond or other asset. Duration is a measure of the price sensitivity of an asset or portfolio to a change in interest rates. The larger the duration of the bond the greater the price risk.

Embedded options: Embedded options tend to be conversion features in securities which gives the issuer or the holder the right but not the obligation to exercise certain rights (such as early repayment etc.).

Financial risk: The probability that the actual financial outcome will be different from the expected outcome.

Fixed-rate instrument: Financial instrument bearing a coupon that is fixed over its life.

Floating-rate note: A note on which the interest rate is periodically reset in accordance with short-term interest rates.

Floor: To set a lower limit on the interest rate to be paid.

Hedge: A transaction undertaken in order to reduce the risk of adverse price movements in a security, by taking a position in a related security or derivative.

Immunization of a portfolio: The process of protecting against interest rate risk by holding asset and liability portfolios of equal duration.

Inflation-indexed bond: A bond on which the nominal return is adjusted by the movement in a specific price index (such as an overall consumer price index). If the security is held to maturity the investor is guaranteed a return higher than the rate of inflation.

Interest rate parity: Where the interest rate differential between two countries is equal to the difference between the forward foreign exchange rate and the spot rate.

Interest rate risk: The possibility of a reduction in the value of a security, especially a fixed-income security, as a result of a rise in interest rates.

Interest rate swap: A contractual agreement between two parties to exchange floating rate payments for fixed-rate payments in the same currency for a stated period of time. When combined with an asset or a liability, a swap can change the risk characteristics of that asset or liability by changing the nature and timing of the cash flows. For example, a floating-rate liability can be converted to a fixed-rate liability using an interest rate swap.

International Swaps and Derivatives Association (ISDA): A self regulatory organization that establishes rules and regulations to promote uniform practices in the writing, trading and settlement of swaps and other derivatives.

LIBOR: The London Interbank Offered Rate represents the rate of interest that major international banks in London charge each other for borrowings.

Liquidity Risk: There are two types of 'liquidity risk.' One refers to the cost or penalty investors face in trying to exit a position when the number of transactors have markedly decreased or because of the lack of depth of a particular market. The other form of liquidity risk, for a borrower, refers to a situation where the volume of liquid assets can diminish quickly in the face of unanticipated cash flow obligations and/or a possible difficulty in raising cash through borrowing in a short period of time.

Marking to Market: Expressing assets and liabilities at current market values.

Market Risk: Also referred to as systematic risk, is the risk of holding a financial exposure whose price may change because of changes in general market conditions.

Matched Position: A situation where the cash flow obligations in a debt portfolio are matched by equally offsetting cash flows in an asset portfolio so that overall value is unaffected by changes in interest rates.

Multi-price Auction: Also know as a discriminatory price auction, where each successful bidder pays the bid price.

Normal distribution: A probability distribution which is a bell-curve in shape and reflects the statistical characteristics of many different types of populations and natural phenomena.

Passive management: A portfolio strategy which seeks to match the risk and return characteristics to an index by mirroring its composition.

Plain vanilla financial instruments: The standard or simplest version of a financial instrument or risk management product.

Primary budget balance: The budget balance excluding interest payments.

Puttable bond: A bond which enables the investor to sell the bond back to the issuer, usually at par, on certain dates prior to maturity.

Put option: Put options provide the holder with the right, but not the obligation, to sell a prescribed amount of a particular security to the writer of the option, at a specified price within a predetermined time period (up to the expiration date).

Repurchase agreement (repo): An agreement in which one party sells a security to another party and agrees to repurchase it on a specified date for a specified price.

Spread: The difference between the yields or prices of similar types of financial instruments.

Strike price: The price at which an option buyer has the right to purchase the underlying instrument.

Tap sales of bonds: Where the issuer sells securities (usually at a fixed price) over a specified period.

Time inconsistency: A situation where policy makers have an incentive to renege on a pre-announced policy commitment after the private sector has made decisions on the basis that policy will not change, even though no news has emerged.

Uniform price auction: Also known as a Dutch auction in which each successful bidder pays the same price—which is usually the price of the lowest successful bidder.

Whipsawed: Loosing money in a volatile market by buying assets before rapid price declines and selling assets before rapid price increases.

Yield curve: A graphical depiction of the relationship between the yield on bonds of the same credit quality but different maturities. Yields on debt instruments which are of lower credit quality are expressed in terms of a spread differential to the default free curve (when the government has a triple A rating in its own currency the default free curve is usually the government yield curve).

Zero coupon bond: Bond issued on a discount basis, so that all payments of principal and interest are deferred until maturity.

Summary of the Debt Management Guidelines[1]

1. DEBT MANAGEMENT OBJECTIVES AND COORDINATION

1.1 Objectives

The main objective of public debt management is to ensure that the government's financing needs and its payment obligations are met at the lowest possible cost over the medium- to long-run, consistent with a prudent degree of risk.

1.2 Scope

Debt management should encompass the main financial obligations over which the central government exercises control.

1.3 Coordination with monetary and fiscal policies

Debt managers, fiscal policy advisors, and central bankers should share an understanding of the objectives of debt management, fiscal, and monetary policies given the interdependencies between their different policy instruments. Debt managers should convey to fiscal authorities their views on the costs and risks associated with government financing requirements and debt levels.

[1]Prepared by the staffs of the World Bank and the International Monetary Fund.

Where the level of financial development allows, there should be a separation of debt management and monetary policy objectives and accountabilities.

Debt management, fiscal, and monetary authorities should share information on the government's current and future liquidity needs.

Debt managers should inform the government on a timely basis of any emerging debt sustainability problems.

2. TRANSPARENCY AND ACCOUNTABILITY

2.1 Clarity of roles, responsibilities and objectives of financial agencies responsible for debt management

The allocation of responsibilities among the ministry of finance, the central bank, or a separate debt management agency, for debt management policy advice, and for undertaking primary debt issues, secondary market arrangements, depository facilities, and clearing and settlement arrangements for trade in government securities, should be publicly disclosed.

The objectives for debt management should be clearly defined and publicly disclosed, and the measures of cost and risk that are adopted should be explained.

2.2 Open process for formulating and reporting of debt management policies

Materially important aspects of debt management operations should be publicly disclosed.

2.3 Public availability of information on debt management policies

The public should be provided with information on the past, current, and projected fiscal activity and consolidated financial position of the government.

The government should regularly publish information on the stock and composition of its debt and financial assets, including their currency, maturity, and interest rate structure.

2.4 Accountability and assurances of integrity by agencies responsible for debt management

Debt management activities should be audited annually by external auditors.

3. INSTITUTIONAL FRAMEWORK

3.1 Governance

The legal framework should clarify the authority to borrow and to issue new debt, invest, and undertake transactions on the government's behalf.

The organizational framework for debt management should be well specified, and ensure that mandates and roles are well articulated.

3.2 Management of internal operations

Risks of government losses from inadequate operational controls should be managed according to sound business practices, including well-articulated responsibilities for staff, and clear monitoring and control policies and reporting arrangements.

Debt management activities should be supported by an accurate and comprehensive management information system with proper safeguards.

Staff involved in debt management should be subject to a code-of-conduct and conflict-of-interest guidelines regarding the management of their personal financial affairs.

Sound business recovery procedures should be in place to mitigate the risk that debt management activities might be severely disrupted by natural disasters, social unrest, or acts of terrorism.

Debt managers should make sure that they receive appropriate legal advice and that the transactions they undertake incorporate sound legal features.

4. DEBT MANAGEMENT STRATEGY

The risks inherent in the structure of the government's debt should be carefully monitored and evaluated. These risks should be mitigated to the extent feasible by modifying the debt structure, taking into account the cost of doing so.

In order to help guide borrowing decisions and reduce the government's risk, debt managers should consider the financial and other risk characteristics of the government's cash flows.

Debt managers should take into account the risks associated with foreign currency and short-term or floating rate debt.

There should be cost-effective cash management policies in place to enable the authorities to meet with a high degree of certainty their financial obligations as they fall due.

5.   RISK MANAGEMENT FRAMEWORK

A framework should be developed to enable debt managers to identify and manage the trade-offs between expected cost and risk in the government debt portfolio.

To assess risk, debt managers should regularly conduct stress tests of the debt portfolio on the basis of the economic and financial shocks to which the government—and the country more generally—are potentially exposed.

5.1   Scope for active management

Debt managers who seek to actively manage the debt portfolio to profit from expectations of movements in interest rates and exchange rates, which differ from those implicit in current market prices, should be aware of the risks involved and accountable for their actions.

5.2   Contingent liabilities

Debt managers should consider the impact that contingent liabilities have on the government's financial position, including its overall liquidity, when making borrowing decisions.

6.   DEVELOPMENT AND MAINTENANCE OF AN EFFICIENT MARKET FOR GOVERNMENT SECURITIES

In order to minimize cost and risk over the medium- to long-run, debt managers should ensure that their policies and operations are consistent with the development of an efficient government securities market.

6.1 Portfolio diversification and instruments

The government should strive to achieve a broad investor base for its domestic and foreign obligations, with due regard to cost and risk, and should treat investors equitably.

6.2 Primary market

Debt management operations in the primary market should be transparent and predictable.

To the extent possible, debt issuance should use market-based mechanisms, including competitive auctions and syndications.

6.3 Secondary market

Governments and central banks should promote the development of resilient secondary markets that can function effectively under a wide range of market conditions.

The systems used to settle and clear financial market transactions involving government securities should reflect sound practices.

References

Alesina, Alberto, Ricardo Hausmann, Rudolf Hommes, and Ernesto Stein. 1999. "Budget Institutions and Fiscal Performance in Latin America." Working Paper Series 394. Inter-American Development Bank, Washington, D.C.

Alexander, William E., Tomás J. T. Baliño, and Charles Enoch. 1995. "The Adoption of Indirect Instruments of Monetary Policy." IMF Occasional Paper 126. Washington, D.C.

Ball, Laurence, and N. Gregory Mankiw. 1995. "What Do Budget Deficits Do?" Prepared for the Federal Reserve Bank of Kansas City Symposium on Budget Deficits and Debt, Jackson Hole, Wyo., August 31–September 2.

Bank of England. 1995. "Report of the Board of Banking Supervision Inquiry into the Circumstances of the Collapse of Barings." July 18. London.

Barro, Robert J. 1998. *Determinants of Economic Growth, A Cross-Country Empirical Study.* Cambridge, Mass.: MIT Press.

BIS (Bank for International Settlements), Committee on the Global Financial System. 1999. "How Should We Design Deep and Liquid Markets? The Case of Government Securities." October. Basel.

Bordo, Michael, Barry Eichengreen, Daniela Klingebiel, and Maria Soledad Martinez-Peria. 2001. "Is the Crisis Problem Growing More Severe?" *Economic Policy* 16 (32, April): 51–82.

Bryant, Ralph C. 2003. *Turbulent Waters, Cross-Border Finance and International Governance.* Washington, D.C.: Brookings Institution Press.

Caselli, Francesco, Alberto Giovannini, and Timothy Lane. 1998. "Fiscal Discipline and the Cost of Public Debt Service: Some Estimates for OECD Countries." IMF Working Paper WP/98/55. International Monetary Fund, Washington, D.C.

Chouraqui, Jean-Claude, Brian Jones, and Robert Bruce Montador. 1986. "Public Debt in a Medium-Term Context and Its Implications for Fiscal Policy." OECD Department of Economics and Statistics Working Paper 30. Organisation for Economic Co-operation and Development, Paris.

Cooper, R. N. 1999. "The Asian Crisis: Causes and Consequences." In Alison Harwood, Robert E. Litan, and Michael Pomerleano, eds., *Financial Markets and Development: The Crisis in Emerging Markets.* Washington, D.C.: Brookings Institution Press.

Currie, Elizabeth, and Antonio Velandia. 1999. "Risk Management of Contingent Liabilities within a Sovereign Asset-Liability Framework." Presented to the Regional Conference on Fiscal Policy, organized by the United Nations Economic Commission on Latin America and the Caribbean (ECLAC), Santiago.

Dixit, Avinash K., and Robert S. Pindyck. 1994. *Investment under Uncertainty.* Princeton, N.J.: Princeton University Press.

Dooley, Michael P. 2000. "Debt and Asset Managers and Financial Crises: Sellers Beware." In Marcel Cassard and David Folkerts-Landau, eds., *Sovereign Assets and Liabilities Management.* Proceedings of a conference held in Hong Kong SAR. Washington, D.C.: International Monetary Fund.

Easterly, William. 1999. "When Is Fiscal Adjustment an Illusion?" Policy Research Working Paper Series 2109. World Bank, Macroeconomics and Growth, Development Research Group, Washington, D.C.

Edwards, Sebastián. 1984. "The Order of Liberalization of the External Sector in Developing Countries." Princeton Essays in International Finance 156. Princeton University, Princeton, N.J.

————. 1999. "On Crisis Prevention: Lessons from Mexico and East Asia." In Alison Harwood, Robert E. Litan, and Michael Pomerleano, eds., *Financial Markets and Development: The Crisis in Emerging Markets.* Washington, D.C.: Brookings Institution Press.

Eichengreen, Barry, Michael Mussa, and others. 1998. "Capital Account Liberalization: Theoretical and Practical Aspects." IMF Occasional Paper 172. International Monetary Fund, Washington, D.C.

Favero, Carlo, Alessandro Missale, and Gustavo Piga. 2000. "EMU and Public Debt Management: One Money, One Debt?" CEPR Policy Paper 3. Centre for Economic Policy Research, London.

Gavin, Michael, Ricardo Hausmann, R. Perotti, and E. Talvi. 1996. "Managing Fiscal Policy in Latin America and the Caribbean: Volatility, Procyclicality, and Limited Creditworthiness." Working Paper Series 325. Office of the Chief Economist, Inter-American Development Bank, Washington, D.C.

Goodhart, C. 1998. "Monetary Policy and Debt Management in the United Kingdom: Some Historical Viewpoints." In "Government Debt Structure and Monetary Conditions," report of a conference organized by the Bank of England, June 18–19.

Hausmann, Ricardo, and Michael Gavin. 1995. "The Roots of Banking Crises: The Macroeconomic Context." Working Paper Series 318. Inter-American Development Bank, Washington, D.C. Processed.

Honohan, Patrick, and Daniela Klingebiel. 2003. "The Fiscal Cost Implications of an Accommodating Approach to Banking Crises." *Journal of Banking and Finance* 27 (8): 1539–60.

IMF (International Monetary Fund). 2000. "Debt- and Reserve-Related Indicators of External Vulnerability." SM/00/65. Washington, D.C.

Jensen, Michael C., and William H. Meckling. 1976. "Theory of the Firm: Managerial Behavior, Agency Costs, and Ownership Structure." *Journal of Financial Economics* 3 (October): 305–60.

Kamin, Steven B., John W. Schindler, and Shawna L. Samuel. 2001. "The Contribution of Domestic and External Factors to Emerging Market Devaluation Crises: An Early Warning Systems Approach." International Finance Discussion Paper 2001-711. Board of Governors of the Federal Reserve System, Washington, D.C.

Kharas, Homi, and Deepak Mishra. 2001. "Fiscal Policy, Hidden Deficits, and Currency Crises." In Shantayanan Devarajan, F. Halsey Rogers, and Lyn Squire, eds., *World Bank Economists' Forum*, vol. 1. Washington, D.C.: World Bank.

Mishkin, Frederic S. 1999. "Lessons from the Tequila Crisis." *Journal of Banking and Finance* 23 (October): 1521–33.

Missale, Alessandro. 1997. "Managing the Public Debt: The Optimal Taxation Approach." *Journal of Economic Surveys* 11 (3, September): 235–65.

———. 1999. *Public Debt Management*. New York: Oxford University Press.

OECD (Organisation for Economic Co-operation and Development). 1988. "Why Economic Policies Change Course: Eleven Case Studies." Paris.

Okonjo-Iweala, Ngozi, Charles C. Soludo, and Mansur Muhtar, eds. 2003. *The Debt Trap in Nigeria: Towards a Sustainable Debt Strategy*. Lawrenceville, N.J.: Africa World Press.

Pålsson, Anne-Marie. 1996. "Does the Degree of Relative Risk Aversion Vary with Household Characteristics?" *Journal of Economic Psychology* 17 (6, December): 771–87.

Polackova, Hana. 1998. "Government Contingent Liabilities: A Hidden Risk to Fiscal Stability." Policy Research Working Paper Series 1989. World Bank, Europe and Central Asia, Poverty Reduction and Economic Management Section Unit, Washington, D.C.

Scott, Graham. 2001. *Public Management in New Zealand—Lessons and Challenges*. New Zealand Business Roundtable.

Smith, C. W., Jr., C. W. Smithson, and D. S. Wilord. 1990. "Five Reasons Why Companies Should Manage Risk." In R. J. Schwartz and C. W. Smith, Jr., eds., *The Handbook of Currency and Interest Rate Risk Management.* New York Institute of Finance.

Sundararajan, V., Hans J. Blommestein, Peter Dattels, Ian S. McCarthy, and Marta Castello-Branco. 1994. "The Coordination of Domestic Public Debt and Monetary Management in Economies in Transition: Issues and Lessons from Experience." IMF Working Paper WP/94/148. International Monetary Fund, Washington, D.C.

Turner, P. 2003. "Bond Market Development: What Are the Policy Issues?" Prepared for a joint World Bank/IMF/Brookings Institution conference on the Future of Domestic Capital Markets in Developing Countries, April 14–16, Washington, D.C.

White, W. R. 2000. "What Have We Learned from Recent Financial Crises and Policy Responses?" BIS Working Paper 84. Bank for International Settlements, Basel.

World Bank. 2000a. "East Asia: From Recovery to Sustained Growth. An Update by the Vice President, East Asia and Pacific Region." March 22. Washington, D.C.

———. 2000b. *Global Economic Prospects and the Developing Countries 2000.* Washington, D.C.

World Bank and IMF (International Monetary Fund). 2001. "Guidelines for Public Debt Management." April. Washington, D.C.

Index

Tables, figures, boxes, and notes are indicated by *t*, *f*, *b*, and *n* respectively.

concentration of responsibilities in,
60–61
contingent liabilities,
responsibilities for, 32,
107–109
contribution to broader perspective
on government balance sheet,
64–69
ethics and, 73–74
fiscal policy advisors, role
compared, 5
forecasts role of, 31–32
interaction with fiscal policy
advisers, 31–32, 47n9
legislative provisions for
establishing, 53, 53b4
location of, 47n8, 61–64
ministry of finance, relationship to,
61–64
organization of, 69–72
personal views of managers as basis
for trading, 94–96
primary objectives, 14–15t2
debt-recording systems. *See*
management information
systems
debt-servicing costs
borrowing in low-coupon foreign
currencies and, 35
cost of debt and, 79
deficits and, 27
during economic shocks, 80
fixed-rate debt, 81
inflation-indexed or variable-rate
debt, 81
price-indexed debt, 145
relation to fiscal aggregates, 49
scenario analysis for, 174
strategy to control, 6, 13, 37,
107, 173
time-inconsistent strategies and,
35, 81
Debt Strategy Module, 130

Debt Sustainability Model, 171
decisionmaking, 18–19, 37, 39,
79, 160
default
avoiding, 15–16
causes of, 14, 28
of counterparty, 99–100
defined, 23n11
foreign currency debt and,
15, 23n11
longitudinal ratings migration
matrices and, 99
risk tolerance and, 79
short-term debt leading to, 15, 18
deficits, 5–6
borrowing from central banks
for, 44
debt-servicing costs and, 27, 46n4
net government indebtedness
and, 26
prolonged, effect of, 27, 46n3, 47n7
understatement of, 10b1
defining government debt
management, 4–5
delegation of authority, 55–56, 74n3,
165–166
demand-and-supply-side shocks, 11
Denmark
central bank's role, 47n11
foreign currency borrowing and,
33, 124n2
government bond issuance, 157n16
government debt management
approach of, 22n4
interdepartmental committees, use
of, 58
deregulation, 3, 22n3, 152–153
derivatives, 18, 97, 120
designing debt management strategy,
17–18
developing countries
See also specific countries
banking crises and, 30

Ireland (*continued*)
liquidity management in, 32
macroeconomic policy setting of,
48n16
middle office in, 71
National Treasury Management
Agency, 55, 57, 61, 74n4,
140n5
nonresident ownership of domestic
bonds of, 157n18
outside experts, use of, 75n7
tactical trading, 96, 117
Israel and price-indexed debt, 156n9

Japanese foreign currency borrowing,
33, 118
joint-venture arrangements with
private investors, 84

Korea, Republic of. *See* East Asian
financial crisis of 1997-98

Latin America
See also specific country
financial crisis in, 29, 30b2, 89
price-indexed debt, 146–147
ratio of public debt to GDP, 26,
46n2
least-risk currency choice, statistical
analysis for, 88
legal requirements of debt
management, 11b1, 50–54
autonomous debt management
agency and, 53, 53b4
capacity-building program and, 165
common elements in developing
countries, 51, 52b3
delegation of authority, 55–56
disclosure of objectives and
responsibilities, 55
requiring prudent fiscal
management, 42

LIBOR (London interbank offered
rate), 82, 102n4, 139n1
liquidity
flow, 32, 147
management, 32, 41
premium, objective to reduce
amount of, 6, 11, 13
risk, 8t1, 98, 148, 174
literature review on optimal structure
of government debt, 79–81
loans
financial intermediaries, 82–83
guarantees, 10b1
maturity mismatches, 82
location of debt management office,
61–64
London interbank offered rate
(LIBOR), 82, 102n4, 139n1
longer-maturity fixed-rate
instruments, 37
longer-term vs. short-term rates,
17, 54
Long Term Capital Management,
near failure of, 94

Maastricht criteria and move to
common currency and central
bank, 48n16
Macroeconomic and Financial
Management Institute of
Eastern and Southern Africa
(MEFMI), 22n4
macroeconomic policy
See also policies, interrelationships of
concerns over, raised by large
public debt, 26
contribution to stability of, 8–11
debt management compared, 5–6
domestic government bond markets
and, 152
managing debt management policy
and, 25–48, 160